Praise for *LEAD with Colla*

Lead with Collaboration is a top-notch resource for all educational leaders. Apsey and Gomez share strategies that are purposeful and practical, along with productive ways to build your team and impact your organization.

> —**Dr. Majalise W. Tolan,** superintendent and author of *She Leads: The Women's Guide to a Career in Educational Leadership*

In this immensely practical book, Apsey and Gomez provide experienced and aspiring leaders with daily guidelines for effective collaboration with colleagues, students, and families. These authors practice what they preach by respecting the reader's time, providing practical tools, and focusing on the essentials of educational leadership.

> —**Douglas Reeves,** founder, Creative Leadership Solutions, and author of *Fearless Schools*

Practical, relatable, sustainable ideas that any leader can implement. Jessica and Allyson pull from their decades of combined experience and having led hundreds of staff meetings in *Lead with Collaboration*. If you're an aspiring, new, or veteran school leader, I guarantee you'll be learning something new on every page of this book. Highly recommended!

> —**Adam Welcome,** author, podcaster, international keynote speaker, forever a teacher

Staff meetings—the dreaded two words for teachers and leaders alike! But Allyson and Jessica have taken those two words and created a new way to see these minutes as a time to collaborate and engage all staff. Everyone will find useful tools in this book to breathe new life into their staff meetings in order to hear all voices and truly embrace the idea of collaboration.

> —**Ann McCarty Perez,** director of professional learning, Creative Leadership Solutions, and author of *The Successful Middle School Schedule*

In *Lead with Collaboration,* [...] provide a much-needed roadmap for how leaders can help teams collaborate more effectively! Anytime I can add more tools to my toolbelt, I'm all in, and this book has given me so many great ideas and takeaways. This book is a must-have addition to any professional library!

> —**Todd Nesloney,** director of culture and strategic leadership, TEPSA

Allyson and Jessica have provided us with enjoyable, simple, cooperative, and significant methods for conducting meetings. Their approach not only makes the process of addressing essential content more pleasurable but also brings about transformative outcomes.

> —**Veronica Godinez,** principal

Lead with Collaboration is a must-have book for all leaders ready to up their meeting game! Jessica and Allyson give many easy-to-implement strategies that you can utilize within your organization. Their strategies will engage your staff and change how your next staff meeting looks and feels!

> —**Lynette White,** district and community relations coordinator

Lead with Collaboration will help you transform boring meetings into purpose-driven time. Whether you're looking to build cohesiveness within your team or use data to guide instruction, *Lead with Collaboration* will give you the knowledge and tools you need for success.

> —**Pam Gildersleeve-Hernandez,** experienced superintendent and nonprofit CEO

An indispensable resource that emphasizes the power of human interaction and the art of engaging others. It thoughtfully highlights the value of inclusion, teamwork, and clear communication in shaping successful meetings.

> —**Jerry Almendarez,** superintendent

Lead with Collaboration

A **LEAD** Like a **PIRATE** Guide

LEAD with COLLABORATION

A Complete Guide for TRANSFORMING Staff Meetings

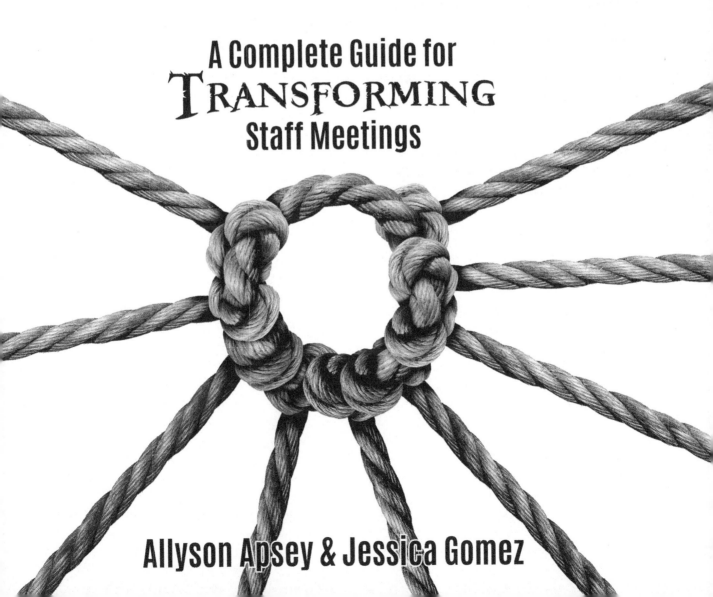

Allyson Apsey & Jessica Gomez

Lead with Collaboration: A Complete Guide for Transforming Staff Meetings
© 2023 Allyson Apsey and Jessica Gomez

This book is available at special discounts when purchased in quantity for educational purposes or for use as premiums, promotions, or fundraisers. For inquiries and details, contact the publisher at books@daveburgessconsulting.com.

Published by Dave Burgess Consulting, Inc.
San Diego, CA
DaveBurgessConsulting.com

Library of Congress Control Number: 2023940356
Paperback ISBN: 978-1-956306-52-1
Ebook ISBN: 978-1-956306-53-8

Cover and interior design by Liz Schreiter
Edited and produced by Reading List Editorial
ReadingListEditorial.com

This book is dedicated to our families. We are so thankful for your continual love and support. Additionally, we would like to thank educational leader colleagues across the country. You inspire us to learn and grow, and for that we are eternally grateful.

Contents

INTRODUCTION

Setting the Stage for Collaboration

> *Collaboration is multiplication.*
>
> —JOHN C. MAXWELL

If you are an educator at any level, chances are you've sat through your share of staff, department, or district meetings. You've probably attended at least one meeting where you learned that a new initiative was going to be implemented but where there was no clear explanation of how it was going to be implemented, nor did anyone ask questions or provide feedback. Information was simply delivered, and it was obvious that the meeting organizers had no intention of hearing from the team. What is the likelihood that you were excited about and looked forward to attending those meetings?

Imagine that you are required to attend a weekly staff meeting in the professional development room. It's meant to be a time for professional learning, collaboration, discussing important updates, giving input on future goals, and addressing any issues that need to be solved as a team. However, you and the rest of your colleagues leave feeling frustrated and unproductive. One week, the principal reviews the latest test scores for thirty minutes without an opportunity for dialogue or collaboration and with no explicit expectations for next steps. Following that, the assistant principal spends ten more minutes talking through the details of a new afterschool program idea, but fails to have a clear plan, budget, or next steps. This leads to an unstructured discussion that goes on for another twenty minutes, with no one able to come up with any decision.

This is an example of a lack of clear communication, goals, and strategies. It is a reminder that staff meetings can easily become unproductive and inefficient when there's no plan, direction, or purpose.

A 2017 *Harvard Business Review* (HBR) article found that 71 percent of 182 senior managers across a range of industries who were surveyed described meetings as unproductive and inefficient.[1] Among educators, staff meetings, as Laura Thomas writes for Edutopia, are often described as "black holes of boring announcements, fruitless debate, and overwhelming agendas, ending in a deeply dissatisfying lack of meaningful conclusions or decisions."[2] Indeed, we have seen firsthand how frustrating and demoralizing it can be for teachers when they feel like their voice is not heard or valued. We also

1 Perlow, Leslie A., Constance Noonan Hadley, and Eunice Eun. "Stop the Meeting Madness." *Harvard Business Review*. June 26, 2017. https://hbr.org/2017/07/stop-the-meeting-madness.
2 Thomas, Laura. "5 Tips for Meetings Worth Going To." Edutopia. George Lucas Educational Foundation. October 18, 2019. https://www.edutopia.org/discussion/5-tips-faculty-meetings-worth-going.

know that meetings are essential for enabling collaboration, creativity, and innovation, that they often foster relationships and ensure proper information exchange, and that they *can* provide real benefits, yet so many meetings fail to fulfill their promise. Why?

Meetings can be experienced negatively due to a variety of reasons. Too often, staff members find meetings boring as they often are talked at versus included in the conversation. This can lead to a lack of engagement and interest, making it challenging for staff members to actively participate. When leaders require face-to-face meetings for content that can be conveyed quickly and does not require extensive discussion, it often leads to the complaint that the meeting could have been an email. Meetings can also be passive in nature, with little interaction between team members. The result is a missed opportunity for meaningful dialogue, collaboration, and trust building.

It is important for educational organizations to be aware of the negative experiences associated with staff meetings and to work toward creating more positive and productive meeting cultures. Reimagining staff meetings as time for teams to learn alongside each other, solve problems together, and inspire one another would be a welcome change for many schools and districts. Doing so could also include involving staff members in the planning and facilitation of meetings, focusing on meaningful discussions and collaboration, and providing opportunities for feedback and follow-up.

To be clear, negative attitudes and experiences do *not* indicate that meetings are wholly unnecessary for modern educators. Sure, we have found that failing to intentionally plan to engage our staff can lead our meetings to become unproductive, mundane, inefficient, and uninspiring. But when planned and implemented well, something as basic as a staff meeting can have significant positive implications for our school sites, departments, and districts.

> When planned and implemented well, something as basic as a staff meeting can have significant positive implications for our school sites, departments, and districts.

In that light, *Lead with Collaboration* serves as a guide for educational leaders looking to incorporate collaboration into their staff meetings, providing step-by-step instructions and ideas that can be easily implemented. These strategies can be used by principals with their staff, by district leaders with principals, and many can even be applied in the classroom. Our approach to this subject is practical, but we also believe that the impact of successful meetings may be profound. Indeed, we believe, on a fundamental level, that meetings can empower educators and create a culture shift that will positively impact teaching and learning throughout schools. We believe that by using fun, collaborative, and meaningful approaches to meetings, we can make the process of covering important content not only more enjoyable, but also transformative.

Our optimism is not without intention, though. We believe that meetings are powerful tools only when they serve as an opportunity to embody and practice the values that we hold as educational leaders. As we will discuss more fully, the most important of those values is collaboration.

MEETING WITH OUR VALUES

The best meetings are those that do not interrupt the great work that we are doing in the classrooms, but instead offer us an opportunity to embrace, and take stock of, our collective educational values so that we can tackle problems and build teams—together. In both form and content, successful meetings serve as powerful opportunities to practice the principles that guide our work every day.

The values that guide educational leaders are as varied as the schools those leaders serve. Throughout *Lead with Collaboration*, we offer techniques and activities that will help your teams to cultivate the following:

- **Authenticity:** Staff members make meaningful connections with one another, valuing and respecting different perspectives, backgrounds, and identities. They communicate openly and honestly with one another, sharing both successes and challenges. Everyone feels safe to be their authentic selves.
- **Enjoyment:** Staff is actively engaged in discussions, sharing ideas and asking questions. There is an upbeat tone where staff display enthusiasm, curiosity, and a sense of humor. The positive energy is contagious.
- **Engagement:** A dynamic environment incorporates collaborative problem-solving and topics that are relevant to the team. Staff members feel comfortable expressing their ideas, challenges, and concerns.
- **Purposefulness:** The meeting's goals and desired outcomes are clearly communicated. The meeting is well organized and structured to make the best use of everyone's time. Agendas address topics that directly relate to the team's responsibilities and the school's overall goals so that discussions are meaningful and valuable.
- **Inclusion:** All staff members feel valued, respected, seen, and heard. There's a welcoming environment where the leader sets the tone of openness, respect, and support. Everyone in the meeting uses language that is respectful and inclusive of all those in the room.
- **Community-building:** The leader creates an atmosphere where staff members feel connected, supported, and engaged in working toward shared goals. Staff feel safe to share their achievements, challenges, and experiences. Teams work together to develop solutions, strategies, or initiatives that positively impact the school's goals.
- **Momentum:** There's motivation and forward movement, and teams feel energized to continue doing the work needed for our students to succeed. Staff members leave a meeting with tangible outcomes and action items to follow up on that create a sense of forward momentum.

- **Accountability:** There is an atmosphere of shared responsibility and ownership for the work. There is a commitment to achieving shared goals and addressing challenges. Meetings revolve around honest feedback, questions, and open communication, fostering a culture of trust, accountability, and continuous improvement.
- **Collective efficacy:** Staff members believe in their ability to work together effectively to achieve shared goals and positively impact student outcomes. The diverse skills and strengths of team members are highlighted, emphasizing how these assets contribute to the collective capacity to achieve goals.

While all of these values are important in their own right, we use the term "collaboration" as a useful index for their cumulative impact. Our passion for collaboration was born from two places, and the first is our desire to set our egos aside and come up with the best outcomes for our students. It is not about us as individual leaders; it is always about "we." Secondly, teachers will be more supportive of systems that they have a hand in creating, and these systems will be better if we listen to the perspectives and expertise of educators.

Collaboration calls upon us to center our team members not just as educators but also as experts. We call teachers professionals, yet if leaders spend time trying to create buy-in by selling new initiatives and programs, they are not treating teachers as the professional educators they truly are. Our goal with collaboration is to shift our culture and practices to ensure that teachers feel like their perspectives, skills, and wisdom are valued and essential to the success of the school. Staff meetings are a great place to start this shift.

Collaboration among school staff yields direct benefits for our students as well. Indeed, research has consistently demonstrated the positive impact of teacher collaboration on student achievement. John Hattie identified "teacher collective efficacy" as having a powerful impact on student achievement.[3] By reinventing how staff meetings are used and fostering a culture of collaboration, we can increase teacher collective efficacy and maximize our impact on student achievement.

A few years ago, one of us suggested to some teachers at our school that we stop having staff meetings altogether and only get together when we needed to dream, problem-solve, or create plans for improvement. They were enthusiastic about this idea and the prospect of elevating all voices during our time together, so we decided to change "staff meetings" to "staff collaboration time" permanently. We have never regretted this decision, and in the chapters of this book, we will share how we incorporate collaboration into all of our work.

---

3   Hattie, John. *Visible Learning for Teachers: Maximizing Impact on Learning*. London: Routledge, 2019.

HOW TO USE THIS BOOK

Lead with Collaboration serves as a complete guide for transforming staff meetings into opportunities for collaboration. We are excited that you join us in having a passion for empowering educator voices during staff, department, and district meetings, and we know that you recognize the powerful cultural transformation that occurs in schools, departments, and districts where leadership is shared and collaboration is the norm. While we focus on strategies that school leaders can implement for designing transformative meetings, this book is not just for principals; it's also an excellent resource for department chairs, professional developers, district administrators, aspiring leaders, college professors, and just about anyone who needs to run a staff meeting and/or collaborative professional development. This is also not a book that needs to be read cover to cover (though you won't want to miss the great ideas in each section) or in sequential order. Feel free to navigate to the sections of the book that speak to your greatest needs.

To mirror how effective staff meetings are set up, the book is divided into three parts. The first part, "Spectacular Starts," highlights strategies for preparing a meeting, how to help everyone feel valued, how to ground the staff in the work they are about to do, and how to build relationships with one another. The second part, "Diving into the Content," centers on ways to incorporate collaboration into the meeting content. The third part of the book, "Ending with Action and Inspiration," focuses on closing meetings in ways that will leave a lasting impact, including ideas for follow-up.

The recent pandemic has caused educators to be creative with staff meetings and professional learning opportunities. Many leaders have discovered the benefits of virtual options, including increased flexibility and access, and are likely to continue using them. To support this shift, we will include ideas for virtual teacher collaboration throughout the book.

At the end of each chapter, we will include a few prompts for readers to reflect and to plan their first steps. Additionally, throughout the book we will reference our website, where leaders can find links to resources, printouts, slideshows, and video tutorials. We are excited to take this journey with you, and we are looking forward to elevating your voice when you share and use the hashtag #LeadwithCollaboration.

As leaders, we know there are many things that we do not have control over. But by planning engaging, collaborative, and meaningful staff meetings, we can improve everything from productivity, communication, and creativity to innovation, greater job satisfaction, and engagement. It is our hope that by the time you finish reading this book you will feel inspired to leverage your unique strengths and talents in order to transform your next staff meeting.

Scan this QR code to access our website leadwithcollaboration.net to find resources that are referenced throughout the book.

Your Next Steps to Set the Stage for Collaboration

What words, ideas, and emotions come to mind when you think about your least successful meeting? Your most successful one?

_____

_____

_____

_____

_____

_____

_____

_____

_____

What are your current meetings like? How could they be better?

_____

_____

_____

_____

_____

_____

_____

_____

_____

_____

PART 1

SPECTACULAR STARTS

CHAPTER 1

Prepping for a Successful Meeting

> *Good luck is when opportunity meets preparation, while bad luck is when lack of preparation meets reality.*
>
> —ELIYAHU GOLDRATT

As a student, Allyson remembers sometimes waking up excited to get ready and go to school to take a test. When this happened, she felt empowered to share the skills and knowledge she had acquired. Other times she would wake up on test days and feel her forehead, hoping that she had a fever and couldn't go to school. There was one distinctive difference between those two types of test anticipation: whether she felt prepared or not. It is the same way when we lead staff meetings.

When we feel like we have a solid agenda that can be accomplished during the allotted time, when the agenda feels aligned with the needs of our students and staff, when we have clearly shared with staff what to expect during the meeting, and when we have all the necessary materials ready to go, we *love* staff meeting day. By contrast, when we scramble at the last minute to pull the agenda together, send it to staff the night before, and are not sure if we will be able to accomplish the outcomes before the staff meeting ends, we *dread* staff meetings.

And preparation is about more than setting the right tone for ourselves; it's also a key factor to making sure that we make the most out of our meetings. Indeed, a major complaint we hear from educators is the lack of time to work together, so we do not have a second of precious meeting time to waste. Preparation is the key to capitalizing on our time together. So, how do we prepare well?

> The success of every meeting hinges on having clear goals and outcomes.

As educators, we know that the devil is in the details, and this holds true for meetings as well. Thankfully, as educators, we have a *lot* of experience in developing highly organized plans for approaching objectives with many contingencies and points of articulation. It can be helpful, then, to think of staff meeting planning like we think of lesson plan development. We expect teachers to have solid plans aligned with curriculum goals that will meet the needs of all of their students. As meeting leaders, it is important that we do the same.

Even as we attend to those details, though, it's crucial that we not lose sight of what matters on a broader scale. The success of every meeting hinges on having clear goals and outcomes. Any meeting that loses sight of its purpose is also likely to lose its audience, resulting in wasted time and frustrated faculty. Purposeful meetings, by contrast, become opportunities for team building, taking on challenges, and making real change.

Purposeful Meetings	Purposeless Meetings
Have visible agendas	Have no clear direction
Have clear outcomes	Lack purpose
Incorporate all voices	Allow a few voices to dominate
Build relationships	Cause unresolved conflict
Leverage collective wisdom	Are one-sided
Result in change	Result in frustration

While every meeting is different, the components included in this chapter can help you to ensure that you've prepared carefully, adequately, and—most importantly—purposefully so that you can set the stage for collaboration.

Author, speaker, and business coach Stephen Lynch has suggested the "Five P's" as a helpful, easy-to-remember framework for successful meetings: purpose, preparation, process, participation, and progress.[1] Three of the Five P's occur before meetings begin. Designating the purpose of the meeting, preparing for a productive meeting, and deciding the most effective process all set the stage for effective collaboration.

SETTING SHARED AGENDAS

Think of the meeting agenda as your personal assistant, and utilize it to its fullest capacity. A good agenda can be used to help structure the timing, flow, and focus of the meeting. Clearly communicating the agenda ahead of time, including the objectives for the meeting, will allow staff the opportunity to give feedback on the agenda and mentally prepare for the meeting. Do not shy away from sending out the meeting slide deck ahead of time; it allows staff to prepare their thoughts and ideas in advance. This can result in a more productive meeting and help utilize the time effectively.

Rather than dictating objectives for the meeting at the outset, try to work toward a shared purpose: find out what staff wants to collaborate about. Send out staff meeting agendas at least several days before the meeting—and be sure to send them out as a draft. For example, if your meeting is on a Friday, send the agenda out on Monday with a message like this:

---

1   Lynch, Stephen. "The 5 P's of Productive Meetings." LinkedIn, June 30, 2021. https://www.linkedin.com/pulse/20140719201013-2338231-the-5-p-s-of-productive-meetings/.

> Hello Team,
>
> Attached is the draft agenda for our staff collaboration time on Friday. It is important that this time together is meaningful for everyone. Please review the draft agenda and let me know what feedback you have.

Nine times out of ten, meeting leaders will not hear any feedback, but even the act of asking can help set the meeting up for success.

A more direct way to find out what staff is interested in learning and collaborating about is to simply ask them. You might approach this in a few different ways:

- Request staff meeting agenda ideas in your staff newsletter a couple weeks ahead of the meeting.
- Send out a Google Form to seek input.
- In conversations with teacher leaders, instructional coaches, and other administrators, make a point to ask them if there is anything they'd like to add to the agenda.

As collaborating on the agenda becomes the norm in your building, teachers and other leaders will begin to seek you out to talk about ideas they have for the next meeting. When determining whether the suggestions that teachers make will work, leaders can consider whether they are priority needs, if they involve the whole staff, and if they could be included on a future agenda if not this one. If staff members suggest agenda items that you decide not to include, be sure to circle back to them and explain why and how the idea they have will be addressed.

A successful agenda incorporates an opening activity that sets the stage for the collaboration, outcomes for the meeting, and a closing activity that includes clarity and action steps. Here is an example of an agenda:

1. Inclusion Activity: Penny for Your Thoughts
   What is on your mind right now?

2. Refresh, Remind, and Renew: Pick and Ask or Tell
   What components of our PBIS plan need refreshing?

3. Analyze Data: Fast and Curious
   How can our recent STAR math data inform our next learning steps?

4. Conclude with Clarity: Your Next Step
   What is your next step based on our meeting today?

5. Follow-Up: Our Next Steps
   What follow-up and action planning should we expect?

This agenda is for a meeting that would last one and a half to two hours. If you have less time, you can divide up agenda items 2 and 3 into different meetings. This agenda outlines the outcomes for each component of the meeting in question format, and it models best practices for the classroom.

During the meeting itself, the agenda can serve as a way to keep purpose in mind for all participants. Have the agenda posted so everyone can see it at all times. In Adaptive Schools training (through Thinking Collaborative),[2] Allyson learned that a visible agenda is like a third perspective in the room, always pointing us back to our goals and purpose. It is especially helpful to reference when an off-topic subject comes up. The leader can say something like, "That is an important topic for future collaboration. Let's put it in our parking lot so we don't forget it." The parking lot can be a spot on a whiteboard or a blank piece of chart paper where you chart ideas, questions, or concerns that come up that are not aligned with the agenda.

PHYSICAL SETUP

Just like when you're setting the dinner table at home for a party, the physical layout of your meeting space is important. Once clear objectives have been established for the meeting, leaders can use the space to help achieve the meeting goals. How we arrange the physical setup sends a message to staff as soon as they walk in the door. Will we work as a whole group today, so the tables are arranged in a horseshoe with teachers sitting around the outside so they face each other? Will teachers work in small collaborative groups, so the tables are spread apart with four chairs at each? Our physical setup speaks to the purpose and agenda before we even say a word, so thinking it through is important.

No matter how long your meeting is scheduled to last, use the environment to create a productive and enjoyable experience that aligns with your meeting focus and goals. Will your meeting involve breakout groups and discussions? If so, the space needs to provide for that. Will your staff need to move around or take notes? In order to take notes, staff members will need a surface to write on. Can everyone be seen and heard clearly? Setting up the space so everyone can turn toward whomever is speaking can help all voices be heard and respected. When determining the most appropriate room setup, consider the focus of the meeting, your staff's comfort, and how to promote learning and collaboration.

Before every meeting, ask yourself these questions to make sure the environment easily lends itself to collaboration:

- Are teams situated where they can talk with one another?
- Is there space to get up and move around the tables for various activities?
- Are there enough chairs for everyone?
- Is there whiteboard space or chart paper available to share group thinking?

---

2   "Adaptive Schools Overview." @ThinkCollab. Accessed February 5, 2023. https://www.thinkingcollaborative.com/workshops-1/adaptive-schools-overview.

VIRTUAL SETUP

The setup is different when meetings are taking place virtually, but it is equally as important to think it through. When they enter the virtual space, what will they see? We may want staff to only see each other's faces when they enter so they can greet each other. Or we might want to have an opening question posted to set the stage for the meeting. Some mood music might help with the initial energy of the meeting. Staff will get a feel for how the meeting will go from the minute they enter the virtual space, and thinking through how we want them to feel will help set the meeting up for success.

What virtual tools could support the anticipated outcomes of the meeting? In some cases, using the chat feature in Zoom and/or breakout rooms might do the trick. In other cases, we may want to use collaboration tools like Google's Jamboard or a versatile tool like Mentimeter that allows for quizzes and open-ended questions. Planning with the outcome in mind will help us choose the right tool for the job. If we want to create a word cloud definition associated with our outcomes, we could use the Mentimeter word cloud feature. If we want to refresh our practices around student engagement, we could use a Jamboard and share what works for each of us. It can get overwhelming because there are so many tools out there, so we recommend picking just two or three to get familiar with to use during virtual meetings.

Virtual meetings sometimes require a bit more administrative maintenance as well. For example, when sending out the agenda for virtual meetings, be sure to share the link to the meeting again. Because new technological features can feel daunting at first, it can be helpful to allow participants to know what the format of the meeting will be and what will be expected of them. This is another good reason to stick with using just a few tools repeatedly during your virtual meetings.

ANTICIPATING NEEDS

Collaboration is only possible when staff members feel comfortable, both emotionally and physically. In that way, preparing for a meeting sometimes means attending to participants' hierarchy of needs. If, for example, staff members come to the meeting hungry after working the whole day, then let's provide them with a little sustenance like fruit, vegetables, and/or crackers and cheese. By contrast, staff members might feel sluggish after lunch, in which case they might need a chocolate pick-me-up. Beyond physical needs, emotional needs are important, too. What will help staff members feel valued and welcomed as they enter the meeting location? We could have tags preprinted with their names so they feel a sense of belonging right away.

Here are some tips and tricks you can use to make sure staff needs are taken care of during the meeting:

- Theme it up! It is always more fun when we tie decorations and refreshments into a theme. You can go simple with something like "Orange you glad it's Staff Collaboration Day?" and have orange decor and orange snacks available. Your theme could be "Spring into Collaboration" with flower decorations and pastel-colored treats. Or you can have staff meeting decor and snacks aligned with your schoolwide theme for the year. Jessica's theme one year was "One Team, One Dream," and meetings had a sports theme each month, like Cracker Jacks and baseball bats for September.

- Hold a "snack potluck." Each grade level brings a snack to share at the staff meeting. Teams can get really creative and bring some delicious goodies.
- Put yourself into a teacher mindset and walk into your meeting space. Is it clear where they are to sit? Can every person see the screen and/or the agenda? Can they easily maneuver out of their seats to head to the restroom when necessary? If using a computer or writing is required, are they able to comfortably do that at a table?

PREPARING MENTALLY

To prepare for a successful staff meeting, it is important not only to plan for a conducive environment, but also to mentally prepare yourself. A positive attitude toward meetings can greatly impact the outcome of the meeting. Instead of viewing meetings as a burden, try reframing your mindset to see them as opportunities for inspiration, collaboration, decision-making, and progress toward goals.

Once you have planned your meeting, visualize it from start to finish, imagining yourself feeling proud and happy after the meeting. This positive visualization can have a significant impact on your success as the meeting facilitator. Consider potential scenarios that may arise during the meeting, and work with a colleague to anticipate and prepare responses for any difficult conversations or questions. Rehearsing these responses will give you the confidence to handle any unexpected situations that may come up during the meeting. If something unexpected happens, and you are unsure of how to respond, inform your team that you need time to evaluate the question or request and will get back to them later.

To ensure successful meetings, think about the atmosphere you want to create and plan accordingly. Good planning and communication before the meeting can foster collaboration and connection among staff. Have confidence in yourself and your abilities, and remember that you were chosen as a leader because you have the skills to guide your team effectively.

TYING IT ALL TOGETHER

- An agenda can serve to organize the meeting by indicating a schedule, outlining the objectives of the meeting, and maintaining the focus of the discussion.
- Thoughtful planning of the physical meeting space is crucial for the meeting's success.
- Consider a meeting space as a way to create a specific experience that will help accomplish the outcomes of the meeting.

- Mentally preparing for your meeting is just as important as setting a clear agenda and a great meeting space.

Your Next Steps in Prepping for a Successful Meeting

Given the purpose of the meeting, and recent events at your school, what might be some of your team's needs?

_____

_____

_____

_____

_____

_____

_____

_____

_____

Think of the purpose you might adopt for an upcoming meeting. What kinds of activities would help you to work toward that goal?

_____

_____

_____

_____

_____

_____

_____

_____

CHAPTER 2
Helping All Staff Feel Included and Valued

> *It is the long history of humankind (and animal kind, too) that those who learned to collaborate and improvise most effectively have prevailed.*
>
> —CHARLES DARWIN

Why does the mention of "staff meeting" cause groans, loud sighs, and dread? Over and over again, we hear from teachers that they do not find staff meetings valuable. In their experience, they often have staff meetings about things that could have been said in an email. Or they feel that staff meeting topics have no relevance for them. Could we begin to help staff members see meetings as an important time to connect with each other? To renew and define a culture of collaboration? We think we can, and the beginning of our meetings provides a perfect opportunity.

With intentionality, we can start meetings in a manner that invites team members to connect and interact with one another. Because the beginning of a meeting often sets the tone for what follows, inclusion and welcome activities are a quick and easy way to actively help staff begin to feel connected with one another, focus on the purpose of the meeting, and to feel comfortable participating. In order for there to be real benefits to a staff meeting, we must allocate time to ground our team and ensure all voices feel heard and included.

These activities also help team members to transition between the activities they just came from and the space they are now in. According to Group Works, "The intention to help people feel welcome and invited to actively contribute grows from an understanding that learning and working together is as much a social process, as a task-oriented one."[1]

When we build relationships, we build community. Building community supports collaborative learning and work. So, while inclusion and welcome activities might not *seem* to be a critical part of a meeting, they can go a long way to making a staff member feel like they belong and increase engagement for the work to come. Additionally, inclusion/

> **When we build relationships, we build community.**

---

1 "Opening and Welcome." Group Works. Accessed February 5, 2023. https://groupworksdeck.org/patterns/Opening_and_Welcome.

welcome activities make meetings more fun without taking up too much time. It's about building relationships with one another.

We both have experienced staff meetings where teachers come in with little to no energy, feeling defeated by the day. We have also both experienced staff meetings where teachers enter wound up and almost slaphappy. Changing the way your team and your organization approach meetings is possible. Altering something as simple as intentionally incorporating inclusion and welcome activities into your meeting can have far-reaching implications. A quick five-minute activity can completely change the vibe of the meeting and the mindset of teachers, whether we need to bring the energy up or calm the room a bit.

CONSIDERING GROUP DYNAMICS

Meeting openings are likely to feel forced when we do not first consider team dynamics that are already at play. However, when we consider how our teams are already relating—with each other, with leaders, and with the tasks at hand—we can leverage inclusion and welcome activities as opportunities to begin purposefully and productively.

Icebreakers have a bad reputation that is earned; even the mention of the term can cause eyes to roll. Why is this, when we know that an engagement activity that happens at the beginning of the meeting can serve such an important purpose? In some cases, it might be because the ice is already broken. If a leader needs to stop energetic conversation to start the meeting with an icebreaker, that is a sign that there is not much ice in the room. In these cases, we suggest reaching for intentional inclusion activities, as outlined below, in lieu of icebreakers.

That being said, icebreakers can be great when the ice in the room *needs* to be broken, like at the beginning of the school year or when there are several new staff members. For groups like these, though, icebreakers still need to contribute toward the larger purpose of a meeting. This will help them to avoid feeling like exercises that force staff into uncomfortable intimacy, or interrupt authentic relationships that already exist. It is always helpful to be transparent about the purpose of the activity, and leaders could put the purpose right on the agenda.

The best inclusion and welcome activities are intentional and tied to a goal, like relationship-building, introducing the content of the meeting, or energizing the room. From high-energy games to quiet conversations to using a technology tool to share staff responses on a screen, varying the types of inclusion and welcome activities can help staff stay engaged.

DEVELOPING COLLECTIVE COMMITMENTS

Rather than viewing the beginning of a meeting as somehow separate from the "real business" that follows, it's crucial to think of opening activities as an intentional statement of vision and purpose. We know that our students feel safest in environments that are predictable and where there are articulated and upheld expectations and roles for everyone. Like with so many things, adults are the same way. Staff members feel most comfortable when they know that meetings are safe spaces where all voices will be included and valued.

Beyond setting tone, opening activities can act as a way to center collaboration from the outset. Establishing meeting norms is an important step in making sure that everyone agrees on how the team will interact and collaborate at meetings. For that reason, we like to frame our norms as "collective commitments," and they often include agreements to provide everyone an opportunity to talk, to be open to new ideas, to value everyone's perspective, and to willingly share ideas.

One way to facilitate this discussion among team members is to start by asking them what they need from other team members during meetings. Have staff spend time reflecting on what they need to truly collaborate by writing their thoughts down on a notecard. They can share their thoughts with each other by doing an idea swap. (More about this shortly.) After they share their collective commitment ideas with each other, they can submit the collective commitment they feel strongest about through a Google Form or some other technology platform. This can lead to the collective commitments of the group.

INCLUSION ACTIVITIES

ONE WORD

Implementation Scenario: When you need to provide context for the meeting's topic and help get everyone in the right mindset for discussion.

- In small groups, ask each person to share one word that comes to mind in relation to the meeting topic or content. There are a few different ways they can share these words with the larger group, such as:
  - Doing a quick round-robin share out of their word, depending on the size of the group and the amount of time you have.
  - Writing their one word on a sticky note and posting it in a designated location for all to read or using a digital sticky note tool like Jamboard to add their one word.
  - Using a technology tool like Mentimeter to add their one word for all to see in a word cloud or free response.

QUOTES AROUND THE ROOM GALLERY WALK

Implementation Scenario: This is a versatile activity that can be used when we are starting a new initiative, need to refresh our knowledge on an established program or practice, or if we want to brainstorm a topic together.

This activity involves displaying quotes around the room that relate to the content of the meeting and asking participants to add sticky notes with their thoughts and reflections on the quotes. For example, if the meeting is focused on Professional Learning Communities (PLCs), some quotes to display might be:

> "Recognize that a collaborative culture will not be created by chance, or even by invitation . . . you must embed collaborative processes into the routine practices of the school."
>
> —Rick DuFour

> "The most valuable resource that all teachers have is each other. Without collaboration, our growth is limited to our own perspectives."
>
> —Robert John Meehan

> "Collaboration, it turns out, is not a gift from the gods but a skill that requires effort and practice."
>
> —Douglas Reeves

EDUCATIONAL GAMES

Implementation Scenario: This activity could be helpful for when you want to do more with less, and either offer a skill share or simply model resources.

This type of activity involves engaging in a hands-on educational game or activity that could be used with students. For example, if the meeting is focused on mathematics, teams might access a resource document like "Math Fun Card Games" and choose a game to play at their table.[2] The goal of these activities is not only to have fun at the start of the meeting but also to find ways to use the games with students in the classroom.

---

2   Bethany. "The 20+ Best Math Card Games That Are Easy to Learn." Math Geek Mama. July 19, 2015. https://mathgeekmama.com/best-math-card-games/.

TRUE OR FALSE GROUP CHALLENGE

Implementation Scenario: This is a fun activity to refresh our memories about a current practice, and if we include some silly questions, we can get a laugh too.

This activity involves presenting the group with a series of true or false statements about the topic of the meeting. It can be used as a review or pre-assessment of the content and helps to set the stage for the discussion. For example, if the meeting is focused on Positive Behavior Intervention and Supports (PBIS), you could create true/false questions associated with your PBIS initiatives.

PBIS True or False

	Statement	True	False
1	PBIS is a program.		
2	The positive in Positive Behavior Support means that we give out rewards.		
3	PBIS is a three-tiered model beginning with Tier 1 which supports all students.		
4	If we implement PBIS, we will no longer punish students for inappropriate behavior.		
5	PBIS acknowledges students for following the expectations and rules and occurs after students have demonstrated the desired behavior.		

MY WISH

Implementation Scenario: When you want to help the group stay focused on their desired outcomes and ensure that everyone is working toward a common goal, this activity can help the group align their goals for the meeting.

1. After the agenda is shared, each staff member should reflect on what they hope to get out of the meeting (their "wish") and share it with a partner or small group.
2. The leader of the meeting listens carefully to the wishes to ensure they align with the goals of the meeting.
3. Collect these wishes and review them during the meeting while the group is collaborating.

IDEA SWAP

Implementation Scenario: This activity is great for helping staff share ideas and/or reflections with each other.

For this activity:

1. Direct participants to reflect on a particular topic or goal by writing a quick reflection on a notecard.
2. Next, ask participants to get up and find a partner to share their reflections. After they share, partners swap cards.
3. Instruct team members to find new partners and share the reflection on the notecard they are holding.
4. Have participants swap ideas several times before bringing them all together.
5. At the end, participants stand in a circle and share the notecard they are holding and then give it to the rightful owner.

SHOW-AND-TELL BINGO

Implementation Scenario: Use this activity to build momentum by allowing staff members to inspire each other with ideas.

For this activity, use our template to create a show-and-tell board that is aligned with current initiatives or goals. The example included on the next page will help staff share ideas for classroom management and relationship building. It can be used in the beginning of the school year or as a midyear refresher. You can customize this BINGO board to support your staff goals by visiting leadwithcollaboration.net.

Show & Tell BINGO

@ALLYSONAPSEY

A classroom routine that helps keep materials organized:	A classroom routine that minimizes transition time:	A routine to quickly get students into pairs or groups:
The best management idea they have implemented this year:	An activity or experience to help students build relationships:	An activity to help the teacher really know students:
A rule or procedure that contributes to an encouraging and safe classroom culture:	A signal this teacher uses to get students' attention:	A strategy to reteach procedures and routines as the school year progresses:

★ Share ideas with each other to complete one of the bingo boxes.

★ Write down the colleague's name and idea in the box.

★ Make sure to have a different name in each box.

★ When you fill out three boxes in a row (across, down or diagonal), yell out BINGO! to claim your prize.

INCLUSION ACTIVITIES TO BUILD RELATIONSHIPS

NAME BALL

Implementation Scenario: This is a great activity for staff members who do not all know each other's names yet, or when you have new staff members join your team. In this activity, you have staff members stand in a circle.

- Staff members toss the ball to a colleague in the circle, saying the colleague's first and last name loudly as they toss the ball. This continues until all colleagues have had a turn to catch and throw the ball.
- Then, have them do it again following the same pattern and surprise them by tossing in a couple more balls.
- This becomes a loud, chaotic, laughing circle of fun, and it is easily replicable in their classrooms.
- The only rules are that they have to repeat the same pattern for tossing the ball, and they cannot toss it to a colleague on either side of them in the circle.

THREE THINGS IN COMMON

Implementation Scenario: This encourages team bonding, especially for team members who might just be meeting each other for the first time.

- Have staff members get into groups of three, ideally with others they don't normally work with.
- Direct participants to find three things they have in common as quickly as possible.
- Give out a prize to the team who sits down first after they figure out their three things in common and to the teams who come up with something others did not know about them. (Candy bars work well as prizes for this activity.)

FAVORITE THING ABOUT OUR TEAM

Implementation Scenario: This activity helps build community and strengthens relationships by reminding staff members all the great things about their team.

- Ask staff members to spend a few moments listing their favorite things about the school staff.
- They then pick one of their favorite things about the team to share with the group.

- Play inspiring instrumental music in the background as each staff member stands and shares what they value most in the staff.
- Better yet, record them as they share so you can play it for them at another time when they need to be reminded of how much they love each other!

THIS OR THAT?

Implementation Scenario: An icebreaker for when you want to celebrate differences and similarities.

The idea is simple: come up with pairs of opposites and have staff members choose which one they relate to most. You can get fancy and make a slideshow with each pair on a slide, or you can simply shout them out and point to the side of the room they go to for each choice.

For instance, you can point to one side of the room and say, "Salty snacks," and then point to the other side of the room and say, "Sweet snacks." The staff members who prefer salty go in that direction, and the staff members who prefer sweet go in the other direction. Here are some opposites you could use for this activity:

- Sweet/salty
- Mild/spicy
- Summer/winter
- Beach/mountains
- Shopping/hiking
- Confrontational/nonconfrontational
- Pool/ocean
- Appetizer/dessert
- First day of school/last day of school
- Friday/Monday (That one will get a laugh!)

FIRST JOB

Implementation Scenario: Use this activity to help teammates get to know each other and learn from each other.

1. Ask staff members to think back to their first job and a lesson they learned during that job that still serves them today.
2. Have staff members pair up to share with each other. Let them know that they will share their partner's response with the whole group.
3. Circle up to have partners share each other's responses. Not only will they inspire each other with the life lessons they learned in their first jobs, they will make connections and have some laughs as they learn about each other.

INCLUSION ACTIVITIES TO ENERGIZE THE GROUP

STRESS BALL TOSS

Implementation Scenario: This may be best during trying times, or when things are starting to drag near the last quarter of a semester.

1. Begin the meeting with someone holding the stress ball and ask them to announce a win.
2. The person holding the ball then randomly tosses the ball to someone else in the group, and it becomes their turn to share a win.

SMARTIES NOSE STACK

Implementation Scenario: This is a great activity for when you need a quick, fun activity to get staff members laughing and relaxed.

- Give each teacher a sleeve of Smarties candy and have them see how many they can stack on their nose without the stack falling off.
- The staff member who has the highest stack wins the Smarty of the Day award, which could be a bag of Smarties to share with their class.

GROUP TIC-TAC-TOE

Implementation Scenario: This activity is best with groups of fifty people or less, and works great with competitive staff teams. It will result in loud chaos, so be ready for the energy to go up!

1. Give each teacher a tic-tac-toe sheet, or have them draw one themselves.
2. Make half of the group X's and the other half O's. It will be helpful for them to wear a sticker or name tag that designates them as an X or an O.
3. Turn on fun, upbeat music to add to the excitement.
4. Those assigned X's find others who are O's and play a tic-tac-toe game with their partner.
5. The loser becomes a cheerleader, and the winner moves on to find another partner.
6. Play until the last winner is standing. A trophy or a little prize adds to the fun.

WINNER OR LOSER

Implementation Scenario: Use this activity when you need to help staff members find the good in challenging situations.

In this activity, staff members work with a partner or small group to reframe negative experiences as learning opportunities.

1. One staff member shares a true personal or work-related memory that was negative.
2. The partner or group helps to identify the silver lining of the bad experience.
3. The original staff member discusses the same experience again, but this time focusing on only the positive aspects.
4. Then, they switch roles and repeat the process.
5. End by having staff share how it felt to reframe their negative experience.

ONE-HANDED BRACELET

Implementation Scenario: This activity is great for when you want to bring joy and fun to your meeting and get everyone laughing.

- Each player has one minute to thread as many Fruit Loops or Cheerios as possible onto a pipe cleaner, but the catch is that they can only use one hand!
- Once they've finished stringing the cereal, they have to turn the pipe cleaner into a bracelet.
- Optional: Have a prize for the person who has the most cereal on their bracelet.

GROUNDING ACTIVITIES TO HELP SETTLE THE MIND

The success of a group is dependent on comfort and a sense of familiarity among its members. To improve group dynamics and foster a sense of trust, try starting meetings with connection and grounding activities, such as coloring pages and mindfulness practices. These activities can also help staff shift their mindset and mood, allowing them to stay focused and engaged during the meeting. By providing opportunities for staff to relax and refocus, you can create a space for them to be open to new learning and collaboration.

These activities can also serve as a learning tool to help the group work better together. Remember, the process of these activities is more important than the end result. By choosing a grounding activity to begin your meetings, you can facilitate better interaction and create an environment where productivity and creativity can thrive.

PENNY FOR YOUR THOUGHTS

Implementation Scenario: This activity is helpful when team members seem distracted or overwhelmed.

1. Give every person a penny and have them select a partner.

2. The partner says, "Penny for your thoughts," and the other person shares something that is on the top of their mind.
3. Then, the sharer gives their partner their penny as a symbol of putting that thought aside during the meeting so they can focus on the collaboration agenda.
4. Then, the partners switch roles.

ANXIETY PROTOCOL

Implementation Scenario: Use this activity when you need to transform worry into action through thoughtful reflection. This activity was developed by Rebekah Schipper, the executive director of Opportunity Thrive, a nonprofit focused on resilience and wellbeing.

- First ask staff members to make a list of everything they are worried about. Be sure to give them plenty of time to write a comprehensive list. They may even pause and think and then continue writing. Then, they circle only the things that fit these three criteria:
    - It is a real problem, not a perceived problem, and you have evidence to back that up.
    - It is of immediate concern, coming up within the next day or two.
    - It is within your control.
- After they circle only the worries that fit all three criteria, they will end up with one or two things they can make an action plan for resolving.
- End the activity by asking them to share how the exercise impacted their level of anxiety.

MINDFUL COLORING (ADULT COLORING PAGES)

Implementation Scenario: This activity helps clear and calm the mind.

- Unlike the coloring books of our childhood, mindfulness coloring is often more abstract, requires more dexterity, and contains calming illustrations with intricate patterns.
- Mindful coloring helps attention flow away from ourselves and into the present moment. It relaxes the brain, and the low stakes make it pleasurable. It can be as neat or as messy as you choose, and this is one of its relaxing perks.

FIND YOUR BREATH

Implementation Scenario: This activity is helpful when you need to tackle an uncomfortable topic, or when team members seem reactive.

Focusing on your breath is a simple and effective way to calm your nervous system and shift out of the fight-or-flight stress response. There are many ways to start a meeting with some intentional breathing, but here are a few you can try:

- Close your eyes and take three extra slow, deep breaths. Bring the breath in as far as you can on the inhale and as far out as you can on the exhale before starting again.
- Set a timer and engage in ocean breathing, taking long breaths in through your nose and then exhaling out of the mouth. Breath slowly and continuously until the time is up.
- Do a few rounds of a specific breathing technique like box breathing (breathing in for a count of 4, holding for 4, exhaling for 4, holding for 4). This is a little more complicated, but counting gives your mind something to focus on while your body gets the nourishing benefits of your breath.

BREATHS OF GRATITUDE

Implementation Scenario: Use this activity to lift spirits and calm minds.

- Many studies have shown that focusing on what you are grateful for boosts your mood, makes you feel healthier, decreases stress and anxiety, and builds resilience. One gratitude strategy that team members at JumpScale, a company that supports leaders to cultivate healthy, resilient and impactful organizations, use is Breaths of Gratitude.
- Each team member in the meeting names something they feel grateful for, and immediately after each share, everyone takes a big, deep breath in and out together.
- A gratitude practice like this is also a great way to end a meeting, letting your team members name their gratitudes, popcorn style.[3]

TYING IT ALL TOGETHER

- Icebreakers may be more useful at the beginning of the school year or when there are many new staff members, but for the rest of the year, intentional inclusion activities can be more effective.
- It is important for meeting leaders to choose activities that will be comfortable for staff and to be transparent about the purpose of the activity.
- Grounding activities allow staff members to quiet their minds and be present in a meeting by providing an opportunity to focus and engage.
- The process of participating in grounding and inclusion activities is more important than the end result, and they can be used as a tool to build community and allow a space for everyone to feel included and valued.

3   Coberly, Bonnie. "4 Mindfulness Practices to Transform Team Meetings." JumpScale. December 16, 2020. https://www.wejumpscale.com/newsfeed/2020/12/16/mindfulness-to-transform-teams.

Your Next Steps to Helping All Staff Feel Included and Valued

What are the dynamics currently at play in your team? Which activities might help to shift or strengthen those dynamics?

_____

_____

_____

_____

_____

_____

_____

_____

_____

What recent—or regular—events might make it necessary to reach for a grounding activity?

_____

_____

_____

_____

_____

_____

_____

_____

_____

CHAPTER 3

Transforming Groups into Teams

> *A group becomes a team when each member is sure enough of himself and his contribution to praise the skill of the others.*
>
> —NORMAN SHIDLE

Meetings aren't just about solving problems through collaboration; they're also crucial opportunities to help staff move from a group of individual educators to a team working together toward the same purpose. We all have experienced being on various teams. Some of them functioned effectively while others felt like they inhibited effective performance rather than enhanced it. What do effective teams have in common?

From our perspective, successful educational teams work toward what John Hattie calls collective teacher efficacy, which is when teams believe that they can work together to achieve shared goals. According to research completed by the *Harvard Business Review*,[1] highly functional teams not only communicate more and use meetings more strategically, they spend time bonding over nonwork topics. They also bring their authentic selves to work, and they share appreciation frequently. In order to take full advantage of the effect of collective teacher efficacy, then, we must attend to trust building and create opportunities for staff to get to know one another.

It's important to note that there is a difference between a team and a group. As explained by Rick DuFour, a trailblazer in the world of Professional Learning Community (PLC) work, on teams no individual wins unless we all win. That implies that we all have to be working toward the same goal. A key in developing teams is first developing a level of trust that supports all team members in taking risks, exposing vulnerabilities, and sharing ideas.

In that light, this chapter does not include the typical camp-type activities we might envision when we think of team building, such as trust falls/trust walks or the human knot. Those activities tend to feel childish or unprofessional and can undermine the effectiveness of the activity and make it difficult to achieve the desired outcomes. They may also feel irrelevant to the team's goals and the focus of the meeting. Those activities have their place, but we focus instead on some activities that might not be

---

1   Friedman, Ron. "5 Things High-Performing Teams Do Differently." *Harvard Business Review*. October 21, 2021. https://hbr.org/2021/10/5-things-high-performing-teams-do-differently.

typically associated with team building but that are absolutely helpful in building the collective efficacy of the team, like identifying and sharing individual core values and strengths.

Team-building strategies can be especially necessary in a staff meeting when there are issues or challenges that require deeper collaboration and communication among colleagues. For example, if there are new members to a grade level or staff, team-building activities can help to build trust and rapport among team members. Team-building activities are most beneficial when they are tailored to the specific needs of the group and are focused on improving communication, promoting collaboration, and building a shared sense of purpose and identity.

> All teams benefit from learning each other's strengths and learning to value each other.

All teams benefit from learning each other's strengths and learning to value each other. This chapter will provide many different team-building activities that will help your team grow together, and many of them can be used in the classroom with students. The majority of these activities will take twenty minutes or more, so they are to be used when you want to dedicate a significant portion of your meeting to team building. Some of these activities may seem like large commitments of time and energy; however, we believe that any time we spend building up our teams and forming strong, positive relationships is not wasted.

IDENTIFYING INDIVIDUAL CORE VALUES

Implementation Scenario: This activity helps team members identify how they contribute to a group's purpose.

Allyson wrote about the power of staff knowing and sharing each other's core values in her book *Leading the Whole Teacher*.[2] (Visit AllysonApsey.com and find the *Leading the Whole Teacher* page for a slideshow that will guide your staff through this activity.) There, Allyson argued that utilizing Brené Brown's core value identification activity with school staff is a powerful team-building activity. Knowing our own core values creates self-awareness that can help us understand the motivation behind our own behavior. Sharing those core values with each other ensures that we recognize the strengths we each can contribute to our colleagues, our students, and our school culture. It sounds morbid, but one of the best ways to identify our core values is to think of our eulogies. What two values do we want people to say we had as they reflect on our lifetime of impact?

- Using a list of core values, have staff members circle the ones that speak to them.
- Guide them to whittle that list down to five core values that mean the most to them.

---

2   Apsey, Allyson. *Leading the Whole Teacher: Strategies for Supporting the Educators in Your School*. San Diego, CA: Dave Burgess Consulting, Inc., 2022.

- Next, they narrow the five down to their two core values.
- Depending on your school culture, staff members can share their core values with everyone, with a small group, or they can collectively reflect on the benefits of the activity.

There are many self-awareness benefits from identifying our own core values, and the benefits of sharing these with our teams are exponential. When Allyson did the core values activity with her team, for example, a teacher shared that one of of her core values is beauty. Her colleagues understood that she looks at the world differently than they do because her core value is beauty. Instantly her behavior went from feeling like having an eye for criticism to having a strength that we all can utilize.

Keeping individual core values in mind helps us understand the motivation behind our behavior and makes collaboration more effective. With that in mind, continually revisit core values to empower teachers through their strengths throughout the year.

IDENTIFYING SCHOOL CORE VALUES

Implementation Scenario: Use this activity when your school's mission and vision need revision.

Collaboration means bridging—and embracing—the differences between individuals and teams. After sharing our individual core values, challenge your team to identify the school's or district's core values.

1. Provide a list of core values, and in small groups or pairs, have staff members circle all the values they think are key to the school culture.
2. Have them select five from the list of values they circled.
3. From there, they narrow their list down to two core values of the school.
4. Have small groups share out to the large group.
5. Collect the responses to review at another meeting to come to consensus.

Whittling an organization's values down to two will not be an easy task, but the discussion that transpires during the process will benefit the entire team. If your team ends up selecting three or four core values for your school, that is just fine. After identifying them, spend time collaborating on what those core values look like in various places in the school and in various situations, like during parent–teacher conferences or during a conflict between staff members.

As with the activity above, consider how the team will continue to revisit the school's core values throughout the school year, especially when making key decisions that will impact the organization as a whole.

THIRTY-SECOND ELEVATOR STORY

Implementation Scenario: This is helpful for when teams feel lost or overwhelmed by too many good ideas and perspectives.

This is a take on the thirty-second elevator pitch. If a staff member was in an elevator and was asked, "Tell me about your school," what would the staff member say? How might a brief statement about your school vary from one staff member to another? How might it benefit your team to have a consistent thirty-second elevator story about your school? Here are some steps to help your team with this process:

1. Give staff members time to pause and write a few sentences to describe your school. Allow them to share their thinking with a partner and then revisit their sentences to see if they would change anything.
2. Then, staff members form groups of four and again share their description of the school. The group then forms one description all together that combines their ideas and, when shared, takes 20–30 seconds.
3. Each group chooses a representative to share their thirty-second elevator story with the rest of the group.
4. End the activity by asking staff members about the most valuable part of the discussion for them. They can share this with the group verbally, or they can write it on a Jamboard, Mentimeter, or Google Doc.
5. A staff member who has a talent for wordsmithing can take the small-group thirty-second elevator stories and craft them into one cohesive story that represents the collective group thinking. That staff member can share it out for feedback, and when a final draft is determined, it can be printed, framed, and made into bookmarks.

WHAT IS YOUR SUPERPOWER?

Implementation Scenario: Useful for when teams are about to tackle a big project that could come across as intimidating.

Educators are often reluctant to brag about themselves because they are humble and sometimes have not identified their own capabilities. In this activity, teachers are asked to share their greatest strengths.

It is important to give participants time to think about their strengths and which one might benefit their teammates. Some team members may even need help from colleagues to identify their own superpowers.

This exercise is also helpful in establishing go-to people for problem-solving. For example, if a teacher is struggling with fitting in small-group reteaching in math, it is very helpful for them to know which colleague has a strength in this area and is willing to help them.

1. Let staff members know at least a week in advance that they are going to be sharing a "super-power" with their colleagues. Their superpower will be included in a staff helpline list, so staff members will know who to turn to for whatever help they need.
2. Include support staff in this activity so they are empowered through their strengths, too.
3. To make sharing their strengths more comfortable, they can share in small groups and add their superpower to a document.
4. Elicit the help of a tech-savvy person who can turn the staff helpline list into an attractive and easy-to-access document.

NO ONE WOULD EVER GUESS

Implementation Scenario: This activity can be particularly useful when a team is facing challenges or transitions and needs to work together more closely. As the saying goes, "Everyone is fighting a battle you know nothing about."

This is a powerful team-building activity, but it can only be used with a team who is willing to be very vulnerable with one another. Every time we do this activity, many people admit to struggling with anxiety, imposter syndrome, the loss of a loved one, or a similar challenge. The room typically falls silent as they read each other's responses, and often tears start to well up for many. There is also, however, usually a sense of relief that starts to flow through the room as individuals realize they are not alone with their struggles.

1. Ask staff members to share a challenge they are going through or have gone through that no one would ever guess. Make sure they know that their answers will be displayed publicly but not connected to their names.
2. Use a tool like Mentimeter to have staff members share, and put their answers up on the screen one by one.
3. An important next step is to collaborate about what support looks like based upon this information by asking, "Now that we know more about the challenges we all face, how might that impact our work together?" This can lead to an informal discussion about support or to developing a collegial system of support that can be built upon each year.

TYING IT ALL TOGETHER

- Transforming groups into teams requires more than just regular team-building activities.
- Building trust among colleagues and promoting a collective efficacy mindset is crucial for improving student achievement.
- Before conducting team-building activities, it's important to understand the specific needs of the staff and communicate the goals and purpose of the activity clearly.

Your Next Steps in Transforming Groups into Teams

Is it more important for your staff to develop personal connections or to align their values and goals? Based on your answer, which activity from this chapter would you use?

_____

_____

_____

_____

_____

Which team-building activity have you found to be the most effective, and how does that experience align with the ideas presented in this chapter?

_____

_____

_____

_____

_____

_____

_____

CHAPTER 4

Celebrations

> *Success can beget success, and celebrating at work helps to build momentum, improve morale, and make the hard times feel all the more worth it.*
>
> —ANDY PARKER, HEAD OF MARKETING AT LEAPSOME

Chalkbeat notes that "more teachers than usual exited the classroom after last school year [2022], confirming longstanding fears that pandemic-era stresses would prompt an outflow of educators . . . Teacher turnover was at its highest point in at least five years—typically around two percentage points greater than before the pandemic. That implies that in a school with fifty teachers, one more than usual left after last school year."[1]

To counter this daunting trend of teachers leaving education for other fields, there are several strategies that can be implemented at various levels. Increasing teacher salaries and benefits, improving working conditions, and providing greater support and resources can help attract and retain quality teachers. At the school level, creating a positive school culture that values and supports teachers can also help reduce turnover rates. Teachers can take steps to reduce burnout and increase job satisfaction by seeking out support from colleagues and mentors, engaging in self-care activities, and focusing on their personal and professional growth.

According to leapsome.com, "79% of US employees who leave their job do so because of feeling under-appreciated. That's not surprising when you consider that 65% of employees claim they've received no recognition within the last year. 35% explicitly note that this under-appreciation negatively impacts their productivity; and a whopping 78% say they would work harder if only they were given more recognition."[2] These statistics clearly point to the importance of including celebrations into your meetings.

We are human, and we do best when we are acknowledged, seen, heard, and recognized for the good work we do. An organization that has a culture of appreciation will excel, and teams will enjoy working with each other. It's about bringing out the best in people and breathing life into the organization.

---

1 Chalkbeat. "Teacher Turnover Hits New Highs across the U.S." Accessed March 6, 2023. https://www.chalkbeat.org/2023/3/6/23624340/teacher-turnover-leaving-the-profession-quitting-higher-rate.

2 Leapsome Team. "How to Celebrate Success at Work: A Guide for Managers." Leapsome. Accessed February 3, 2023. https://www.leapsome.com/blog/how-to-celebrate-success-at-work.

> An organization that has a culture of appreciation will excel, and teams will enjoy working with each other.

Too often, leaders plow through a staff meeting, focusing only on the business aspect of it, neglecting the personal connection and celebration time needed for our teams to thrive and grow. Celebration honors the work that has been done and shows gratitude to the people who do it.

Being specific about the celebration and/or success and how it made an impact on you or the organization is key to making the celebration authentic and meaningful. Habits and qualities are just as important to celebrate as numbers and targets are. Celebrations connect team members and help others feel included and part of the team.

Celebrations don't have to be long, cumbersome, or complicated. This chapter includes tips and strategies leaders can implement in their staff meetings to acknowledge and recognize staff. The ideas shared will support staff in acknowledging and recognizing one another. Additionally, we give you several ways to continually celebrate throughout the school year, even between meetings.

STRATEGIES FOR CELEBRATING SUCCESSES AND THE TEAM

DIFFERENCE MAKER (REFLECT, WRITE, SHARE)

Implementation Scenario: When you want to give team members an opportunity to be inspired by one another.

This activity not only brings a smile to everyone's face and sets a positive tone and energy for the meeting, it also gives each staff member a few moments to sit and reflect on something that they may not have otherwise taken time to do. It's important for staff to remember the impactful interactions and conversations they have on a day-to-day basis. This helps everyone realize how important they are to the team and that everyone is capable of making a difference.

1. Direct team members to reflect, in groups of three or four, on ways they are difference makers.
2. Ask each person in the group to reflect on a decision, task, or interaction that they felt made an impact.
3. Next, have each group member write some details about the event and then share their story with their group.

"I NOTICED . . ."

Implementation Scenario: This could be useful when team members are having trouble seeing their successes.

1. Ask each person to think about something positive using one of these two sentence starters:
   - "I noticed . . ."
   - "Did you know that . . ."
2. Like in the One Word inclusion activity from earlier, you can use technology tools like Google Jamboard or Mentimeter for all team members' voices to be heard and seen when sharing their "noticings."
3. Choose a few volunteers to share out their "noticings" with the larger group.

KUDOS AND THANK-YOUS

Implementation Scenario: This is a great activity to do at the end of a school year, during Staff Appreciation Week, Principal Appreciation Month, or at the end of a semester.

Jessica experienced the power of this idea firsthand at a district meeting and still has her printed slide hanging in her office. It was Principal Appreciation Month, and her district directors had created slides ahead of time with each principal's picture and name. At the start of the meeting, the district leaders incorporated time for the principals to add their thanks on other principal's slides. It was very heartwarming to see all the kind words that were added to each administrator's slides. A week later, the principals got a surprise in the mail with their slide printed out in color for them to keep. It was a beautiful memento of the hard work principals put in each and every day.

Digital Version:

1. Using Google Jamboard or any other shared collaborative platform that works in a similar fashion, give each team member a preassigned slide with their name and/or picture in the center of the slide. If you have a big team, it would be helpful to set up each slide or frame by team members' last names.
2. If using Google Jamboard, ask staff to thank colleagues on their slides by adding a textbox or a digital sticky note.
3. After the meeting, each slide gets printed for team members to cherish.

Hard-Copy Version:

1. Make a sheet of paper with each staff member's name and/or picture in the center of the slide and hang it around the room.
2. Ask staff to write their thank-yous on colleagues' papers or using sticky notes.

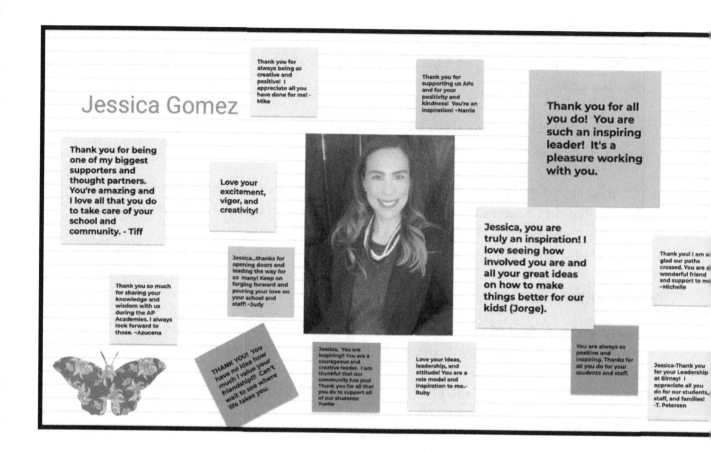

"ALL WE DO IS WIN"

Implementation Scenario: A good one when you need a great energizer to get the team moving and connecting with one another for a few minutes.

1. Ask each team member to find another colleague and share one win.
2. Perform step 1 twice, with two different partners. Give 2–3 minutes for each round.
3. Be clear that staff can share the same win or a different win at each round.

This activity is meant to be quick, easy, and low prep, so limiting the share-out to one win is helpful, but you can certainly modify that as needed. To add a little extra energy to the room, you may consider playing some upbeat music to transition from one round to the next or even keeping it on during the partner share.

LETTER-WRITING PARTY

Implementation Scenario: This can be used at any time in the year but can be especially fun during Christmas or around Valentine's Day, or even during Staff Appreciation Week.

For this activity, you will need blank cards and pens. To add a little extra flair, you can have fun or fancy pens, markers, stickers, or ink pads and stamps.

At the end of your meeting, provide time (5–10 minutes should be plenty) for each person to write 1–2 thank-you cards to a colleague, student, or family member. Afterward, cards can be delivered to the person during or after the meeting.

TEAM CELEBRATION BOARDS

Implementation Scenario: This is a great activity to use at a staff meeting at the end of a month, quarter, semester, or school year as a reminder of the great work each team is doing.

For this activity, you will need markers and poster paper, construction paper, or anything you can use to create a team board.

Direct grade-level teams, department teams, and office teams to design their own boards displaying team wins. They could use writing, drawings, or anything else to represent those wins. The tone could be professional, personal, or both; encourage creativity.

TYING IT ALL TOGETHER

- Celebrating successes, both big and small, is important for creating a culture of appreciation and bringing out the best in people.
- Incorporating celebrations at the beginning of a meeting helps establish a positive tone and inspires the team to keep striving. It also serves as a reminder that their contributions are valued.
- Feeling appreciated and celebrated boosts morale and motivation, so it's important to make time in meetings to express gratitude and celebrate one another's achievements.
- A culture of appreciation fosters a positive and enjoyable work environment, which can lead to increased dedication and effort from the team.
- It's easy to incorporate celebration and appreciation into meetings without making it complicated. Simple gestures can go a long way in making staff meetings more enjoyable and conducive to team success.

Your Next Steps to Celebrate the Team

What was a missed opportunity for celebration this past semester?

_____

_____

_____

_____

_____

_____

_____

_____

_____

_____

How would you like to acknowledge it next time?

_____

_____

_____

_____

_____

_____

_____

_____

_____

_____

PART 2

DIVING INTO THE CONTENT

CHAPTER 5

Making the Mundane Magical

> *I have always tried to live by the "awe principle." That is:
> Can I find awe, wonder and enchantment in the most
> mundane things conceivable?*
>
> —CRAIG HATKOFF

There's no way around it: sometimes, staff meetings need to cover mundane topics. No one gets excited to review the handbook each fall or to go over safety drill procedures once again.

These meat-and-potatoes topics sometimes feel disconnected from the goals, values, and mission of our school sites or organizations. In that light, it's important to emphasize how these topics actually embody our purpose; they give us an opportunity to make sure that we are all on the same page and we are providing consistent expectations for students, families, and staff.

As leaders, it is also our responsibility to ensure that all learning and collaboration in staff meetings is meaningful, even if the topics themselves may not seem particularly exciting. Thankfully, the same inventive, engaging pedagogical techniques that we leverage in order to electrify even the most milquetoast of classroom topics can serve us just as well in the context of staff meetings.

Let's consider what authentic, deep student engagement looks like in the classroom. Dr. Douglas Reeves defines engagement as the "mutually focused attention of students and teachers on curiosity, challenge, and learning."[1] This is the type of engagement we should aim for in every classroom. When students are driven by curiosity, we may see them working together in collaborative conversations or writing while they think deeply.

---

1   Reeves, Douglas B. *Transforming Professional Development into Student Results*. Alexandria, VA: ASCD, 2010.

However, in staff meetings, as in classrooms, we can't always know what others are thinking and when they are feeling engaged. As a result, it's important to communicate verbally and reflect through writing to share ideas and build understanding. Even agenda items that seem purely one-way in terms of information exchange can become opportunities for collaboration. When content is likely to be boring, or feel passive, we need to consider making it interactive, using multimedia, personalizing the experience, encouraging communication, and making it as relevant and meaningful as possible. The techniques in this chapter can make the mundane magical!

> It's important to communicate verbally and reflect through writing to share ideas and build understanding.

PICK AND ASK OR TELL

Implementation Scenario: This is useful for topics where participants know most of the information about subjects and simply need to hone or refresh their knowledge. For example, this activity could be used as a handbook scavenger hunt. The sky is really the limit with this versatile activity, and it can take 20–40 minutes.

1. Fill manila envelopes (one for each small group) with items aligned to the learning or review. For example, Allyson put in items associated with the school Positive Behavior Intervention and Supports (PBIS) and Social-Emotional Learning (SEL) programs. Each envelope will have the same items. If you are using this idea for a staff handbook scavenger hunt, you could fill the envelope with questions about the handbook.

2. Divide staff up into the appropriate number of small groups of 4–6 people, and give each group one manila envelope.

3. Members of each small group pass around the envelope, and one at a time, each person picks an item and tells everything they know about it or asks a question about the item.

Here's a script for you to instruct teams at your meeting:

- Pass the envelope to the right.
- When it is your turn, close your eyes and pick an item from the envelope.
- Tell your group about the item, sharing everything you know about it. Then, ask a question about the item if you have one.
- If you don't know anything about the item, no worries! Just ask your group to teach you about it.
- The person who just went will be the notetaker for the next person's turn, so the notetaking paper will follow the envelope around the circle. Visit leadwithcollaboration.net for a template of the notetaking paper.
- The notetaker will write down the item's name and any lingering questions or ideas the group has about the item.
- We will quickly go through the items when we get back together as a whole group to answer any important questions you may have.

GAMIFY IT!

Implementation Scenario: This activity works great for when you want to keep focus high and the energy light without sacrificing content coverage.

Remember how teachers used to make Jeopardy games with notecards on the board or play Family Feud in their classrooms? Kahoot and other online quiz games can be a great way for teachers to review content with their students, and they can also be useful in staff meetings. Teachers often enjoy friendly competition, and these tools can help facilitate that.

In addition to using online quiz games, you could also try incorporating activities like acting out mundane topics and voting on the best performance. Don't be afraid to try out those old-school methods like the notecard Jeopardy to turn boring concepts into opportunities for laughter and fun in the staff room.

INCORPORATE TECHNOLOGICAL TOOLS

Implementation Scenario: Use technology tools to elevate all voices by allowing staff to share their ideas and thoughts digitally.

To review important content with students, teachers often revisit it in different ways, such as using technology tools. This could be a good opportunity to use Jamboard for sharing ideas or to have groups of teachers create a Google Slide to present a page from the handbook or a procedure. The more creative they can be, the better, as creativity and novelty can make learning more memorable. Plus, it can be enjoyable to get creative together. This is also a good opportunity to model high-tech collaboration tools—the kind teachers can take back to their classes—as well.

MAKE AND TAKE

Implementation Scenario: Use this activity when you want to reinvigorate a school practice that has gradually disappeared or become diluted, or you want to supply teachers with tools for a new initiative.

Whatever area needs a collaborative implementation boost in your classrooms can be the focus of the Make and Take. It is most effective and fun to make this plan with a team so you can divide and conquer.

1. Determine the goal for your time together. Do you want teachers to walk out with everything they need to create a Calm Corner in their classroom? Or do you want to help them have math manipulatives ready for Math Workshop?
2. Set a budget, and don't be afraid to get creative about where the funds will come from. Local businesses, your school's PTO, and other donation sources may want to support this effort.
3. Make a list of what you'd like teachers to walk away with, in these categories:

    a) Make: What will they actually make together, given the time frame you have?
    b) Choices: What items will they be able to choose to empower them to meet the needs of their particular students?
    c) Take: What items will all teachers take with them to ensure consistency in implementation?
    d) Organize: How might you help teachers organize the materials? Would a shoebox-sized carton help them keep all the materials together? Would you want to provide a label for the carton?

4. Create a materials list. We get right on school supply sites or online stores to price things out and place them in our carts. Here are a few categories for materials:

a) Dollar-store items: There are many inexpensive craft supplies at dollar stores. It may take some perseverance because you may have to travel to many to find the supplies you need. Some staff members love to do this!

b) Online-store items: Be careful to watch shipping times with online stores. We always have the best luck with Amazon, but there are many other options.

c) "Raid your cupboard" items: These are items that teachers may have in their cupboards at school, like extra glue sticks, glue guns, ribbon or material, markers, etc. You can send out a list of these items, and teachers can donate right from the extras in their cupboards.

5. Draft a room setup plan so teachers can easily move around and make their items. Think about how to make the event fun and exciting, with music, snacks, and simple decor.

6. Create a fun invitation. For example, one of Allyson's "Make and Take" sessions was designed to create a "Regulation Station," so she made an invite.

"STATE OF THE SCHOOL" ADDRESS

Implementation Scenario: This activity can be used when a leader needs to share information that could raise questions, be emotional, or be misunderstood. This allows all staff to hear the same information at the same time.

It is true that if a meeting could be an email, it should be an email. But there are some exceptions. For instance, if the information may bring up some pretty heavy emotions, or might result in many follow-up questions, it may be best to share it in person.

Allyson had a meeting every year in the early spring called the State of the School Address to share the information she had about current happenings and what to expect in the upcoming year. Every year, staff would begin speculating about possible changes for the next year, and Allyson wanted to share the same information at the same time with all of them. This gave staff an opportunity to ask questions to gain a better understanding of what was known and, sometimes more importantly, what was unknown.

She set the room up like a press conference, with a lectern emblazoned with a State of the School Address emblem. This was intended to create a fun atmosphere and to communicate that, unlike the typical collaboration meetings, this one was more of a "sit and get" type of meeting. Allyson prepared a slideshow with visuals for the information and allowed for questions between each topic. The meeting was always well received and gave Allyson great information about what lingering questions the staff had.

STRETCH TALL OR FOLD FLAT

Implementation Scenario: Use this activity to get staff moving while you process important points of your learning. This will be a great review, and will probably result in some laughs! It's an activity they can take and use in their classroom right away.

1. Have staff members review the handbook, read an article about an initiative, or discuss a topic together.
2. They each write out one true statement and one false statement about the topic.
3. Gather up their statements, ask staff to stand, and then you will read the statements aloud, one at a time.
4. If staff members agree with the statement you read, they stretch up as tall as they can. If they disagree with the statement, they fold flat and touch their toes.

5. Let staff know that accommodations are made at your school, and if they cannot fold all the way down to touch their toes, that is okay.

PAUSE AND PONDER

Implementation Scenario: Use this activity to allow staff members to individually reflect in writing about a meeting topic.

It is important to recognize that some staff members are more comfortable speaking up than others. This is for several reasons, and one reason is that it takes some people longer to collect their thoughts than others. One strategy to help elevate all staff voices and to develop a culture of equity in collaboration is to regularly utilize Pause and Ponder.

To support everyone in thinking through their responses before they share about the meeting topic, allow them time to pause and ponder before they respond. They may need as little as one minute to silently write their thoughts, or, for more complex topics, they may need a few more minutes.

You can make this activity more engaging by using creative notecards, stickers, colorful markers, or fun sticky notes. After they pause and ponder to write down their thoughts, they can share using the Idea Swap strategy from chapter 2.

Pause and Ponder

My first thought is...

_____

_____

Because...

_____

_____

After some reflection, now I think...

_____

_____

_____

#LeadWithCollaboration

USING FUN PROPS

Implementation Scenario: Using a fun prop like a spinning wheel or a huge blow-up dice can make meetings more enjoyable.

Purchasing a spinning wheel, like the ones they have at carnivals, is easier and less expensive than you might think. Allyson purchased a tabletop multicolored wheel from Amazon and has used it for a myriad of purposes. One fun way to make boring meeting topics more fun is to put questions about the topic on the wheel and have staff members come up and give it a spin. Alternatively, you can number topics 1–6 and have each group roll a huge blow-up dice to determine which topic they will focus on. Look for inexpensive props at the dollar store or party store. Something as simple as a plastic top hat can add an element of novelty to a meeting. For example, staff members can draw their partner's name out of the hat for an activity.

TYING IT ALL TOGETHER

- Staff meetings can be transformed from frustrating to valued time when we ensure that the learning and collaboration that happens in them is meaningful, even if the topics themselves may not seem particularly exciting.
- Leaders must model authentic, deep engagement, and communication and reflection through writing can help facilitate understanding in staff meetings.
- Mundane topics are more engaging and collaborative when we incorporate technology tools or get creative with activities.
- It is important to include mundane topics, like reviewing handbooks and policies, in staff meetings, but these topics do not have to be boring and can be made into magical collaboration opportunities.

Your Next Steps to Making the Mundane Magical

What are "problem topics" for your team? What content do you have trouble getting through? What activity from this chapter would help with the problem areas?

_____

_____

_____

_____

_____

_____

_____

_____

By contrast, what content seems well understood but needs to be covered on a regular basis? What activities from this chapter are you considering for these topics?

_____

_____

_____

_____

_____

_____

_____

_____

_____

CHAPTER 6

Learning Together

> *Collaboration allows teachers to capture each other's fund of collective intelligence.*
>
> —MIKE SCHMOKER

Great organizations learn together. When we are resistant to learning and growing together, we risk becoming stagnant and irrelevant instead of being innovative and forward thinking. Everyone (students, staff, community) benefits from focusing on learning together and lifting each other up. When learning together becomes the norm and the culture of the organization, teams are better able to adapt to change and new challenges, which is inevitable in the world of education. When team members learn together, as opposed to being "instructed" by a school leader or outside expert, they are also more likely to feel a sense of unity, camaraderie, and togetherness, which can boost team morale and accomplishments.

We can even approach problems as more open-ended learning opportunities. Reframed in that way, staff members bring different perspectives, which can result in more creative and successful solutions. When given the space and time to collaborate and learn from one another, team members have the opportunity to discuss and exchange ideas, which can improve their instructional craft in ways that are not possible when working in silos.

When it comes time to meet, learning cannot be an act of mere information dissemination; instead, it should be a collaborative process. In an article from George Washington University's Graduate School of Education and Human Development, we find that student collaborative learning, or learning together, has become one of the strongest core philosophies operating in classrooms today.[1] As one nationally board-certified teacher stated, "Peer-to-peer collaboration can turn a small idea into the seeds for something fabulous."[2] Why would it be any different for the adults in our schools and organizations?

---

1 "10 Strategies to Build on Student Collaboration in the Classroom." The Graduate School of Education and Human Development, George Washington University. Accessed February 5, 2023. https://gsehd.gwu.edu/articles/10-strategies-build-student-collaboration-classroom.

2 Gates, Sabrina. "Benefits of Collaboration." NEA. Accessed February 5, 2023. https://www.nea.org/professional-excellence/student-engagement/tools-tips/benefits-collaboration.

When we value learning in our staff meetings, we are building toward the same powerful outcomes we hope to inspire in our classrooms. As collaborative learners, our team members will:

- Develop a shared understanding: Developing a shared understanding within a team can help to ensure that all team members have a clear understanding of the team's goals, objectives, and expectations. This can lead to better alignment of individual efforts toward the team's goals, improved communication, and reduced misunderstandings.

- Increase team collaboration: This can lead to improved creativity, innovation, and problem-solving. When team members collaborate effectively, they can share their knowledge and skills, identify and overcome obstacles, and utilize diverse perspectives to get creative.

- Enhance team problem-solving: When teams work together to solve problems, they are able to leverage their collective intelligence, knowledge, and experience. This can lead to better problem-solving outcomes, increased efficiency and effectiveness, and improved decision-making.

- Improve team and individual motivation: This can lead to better performance, increased engagement, and job satisfaction. When team members feel motivated, they are more likely to put forth their best effort and take ownership of their work, which can lead to better outcomes for the team as a whole.

- Better information retention: When teams work together to learn new information, they are more likely to retain that information over time. This is because team members can help each other to understand and remember important details and can provide reminders and reinforcement to each other as needed. Additionally, team-based learning activities can help to make learning more engaging and memorable for team members.

Learning together can be as much fun and as enjoyable for adults as it is for students because they have the opportunity to interact with their peers or colleagues. In this chapter, readers will discover a collection of new tools at their fingertips.

> When we value learning in our staff meetings, we are building toward the same powerful outcomes we hope to inspire in our classrooms.

THE WORLD CAFÉ

Implementation Scenario: This technique is especially valuable when you need to examine a subject from various angles, ensure active participation from all members during discussions, and promote the generation of fresh insights and connections among participants.

The World Café is a collaborative conversation strategy that is designed to facilitate the exchange of ideas and knowledge among participants, facilitate group discussions and problem-solving, and create a sense of community. The World Café is especially useful for generating many ideas and for encouraging shared understanding among participants.

1. Set up round or rectangular tables, each with a facilitator and a small group of participants, typically 4–5.
2. Designate one member of each group as the table facilitator. This person helps to guide the conversation and ensure that everyone has the opportunity to share their thoughts and ideas.
3. Give each table member a question, topic, or theme for the café that is relevant to the group and that will generate meaningful discussion.
4. After a set amount of time (15–30 minutes), direct participants to rotate to a new table and give them a new question or topic to discuss. The facilitators remain at their original tables.
5. Continue this process for a set number of rounds. After each round, ask staff members to share key insights and concepts that emerged from the discussion.

> For more detailed information and tools for facilitating this strategy, consider visiting theworldcafe.com.[3] You will find specifics and visual examples for how to effectively facilitate this collaborative discussion method.

MISSION POSSIBLE

Implementation Scenario: This could be helpful when teams need to approach an especially challenging goal with which they may have had trouble in the past or if there is uneasiness around a certain initiative. But really, it could be used at any time to mix things up!

Make collaborative learning fun and active by sending your staff on a group scavenger hunt. Mission Possible is a play on the Mission Impossible series of action films that follow the missions of a team of secret agents who are members of the Impossible Missions Force and are tasked with completing high-stakes missions, gathering intelligence, and removing obstacles and threats.

---

3   "World Cafe Method." The World Café. November 25, 2019. https://theworldcafe.com/key-concepts-resources/world-cafe-method/.

In the movies, the team must use their skills and resources to outsmart and outmaneuver their challengers. The Mission Possible strategy works in a similar fashion, underscoring that together we can accomplish anything! For those staff members who love a little competition, this strategy will be right up their alley.

Scan the QR code to access a sample template that can be used to set up your missions.

1. Prior to the staff meeting, set up a series of challenges that teams must complete in a certain amount of time as a team in order to "succeed" in their mission. This could include a shared reading, exploring a website, secret codes, puzzles, problem-solving tasks, and more.

2. Each team's goal is to complete the missions in any order, prepare their mission reports, and then rejoin the whole group, ready to share their findings.

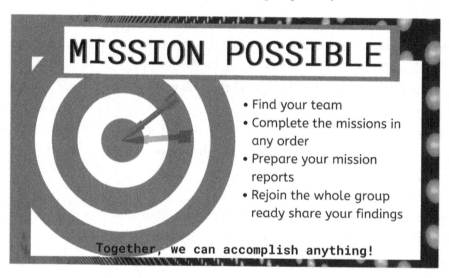

BACK-TO-THE-FUTURE PLANNING

Implementation Scenario: This activity could be especially helpful at the start of the year or whenever you're approaching long-term goals that might seem daunting.

This activity, themed around the eighties film *Back to the Future*, supports staff in purposeful planning by going back to the future. We first dream ahead to the end of the year, to start with the end in mind, and then we work our way backward. This activity can be completed in pairs or small groups before coming together to develop a timeline for implementation.

1. Define the overall goal for your team to center each group's ideation. For instance, are we planning for successful implementation of a new curriculum tool? Or are we planning for a particular student achievement goal? This activity is adaptable to almost any outcome.

2. Divide the group into teams or pairs and ask each team to picture what success in that goal will look, sound, and feel like. That clear picture will drive their planning.

3. Ask each team to identify the starting point for working toward that goal. Once they are clear about where they are starting and where they are going, accurate planning can occur. Wherever they are starting is perfectly fine.

4. Direct each team to break down their vision of success into four smaller goals that are spread throughout the school year. Encourage participants to be realistically ambitious and as specific as possible. They can strategically place the goals on a timeline, keeping the parameters of the school year, breaks, and marking periods in mind.

5. Come back together as a larger group to synthesize the Back to the Future plans into one plan for the school. Create calendar reminders for everyone right then and there to hold each other accountable for each step of the plan.

CHALLENGES TO OPPORTUNITIES

Implementation Scenario: This could be used at the beginning of a school year, a new quarter, new semester, or when embarking on a new school or district initiative.

1. Direct staff to individually brainstorm some of the challenges they may face during a given time frame (i.e., over a quarter or semester) or with a particular initiative.

2. Ask individuals to identify the biggest challenge from their list.

3. Divide staff into groups of three or four. Individuals share their biggest challenge, and they choose one to focus on as a group.

4. Direct each group to use half of a poster, shared paper, or digital workspace like Google Slides to represent their challenge using drawings or images. There should be no writing except to jot down the names of the people in the group.

5. Next, they'll use the other half of the poster to reframe the challenge into an opportunity. Again, they will use drawings and imagery rather than words to represent the opportunity.

6. Each group shares their pictures with the whole group and describes how they reframed their challenge into an opportunity.

SHOW AND TELL

Implementation Scenario: This is great to highlight your team's strengths and skills. When teachers or staff members have experience or expertise in a particular instructional delivery strategy or subject, they can share their knowledge simply by being given the floor.

Like in the classroom, where students bring an object from home to school and share it with the class, talking about its personal significance or interesting features, teachers and staff can do the same with an instructional tool, strategy, or idea.

By allowing time in a meeting for staff to share meaningful strategies or ideas that can easily be replicated, you build community among colleagues, validate the great work of the staff member sharing, and add one more tool to teachers' and staff members' toolboxes.

This should be planned ahead of time so the staff member can prepare what and how they will share out. You can distribute a sign-up sheet for teachers or staff members and/or you could ask a teacher or staff member to share the great idea or strategy that you've observed them using. When doing your classroom and site visits, be on the lookout for those great strategies staff might share at the next staff meeting.

FIVE-MINUTE BITE-SIZED PD

Implementation Scenario: Consider using this strategy when staff meeting time is limited and/ or when implementing a new campus-wide tool or initiative.

Jessica started using this strategy when her school district purchased interactive smart boards for every classroom in the district. Interactive smart boards can make lessons more engaging for students, can be used for collaborative learning, and allow easy access to digital resources, enabling teachers to better customize their lessons and activities to meet the needs of their students.

What Jessica realized was that there had to be some form of continuous learning around how to use the new interactive smart boards if *all* teachers were going to be able to use them to their fullest capacity. Like any new tool, the learning curve can be steeper for some than it is for others. As a result, when Jessica visited classrooms, she started paying attention to all the innovative ways teachers were beginning to use the interactive whiteboards. She asked them if they would be comfortable sharing their whiteboard strategy she just observed at the next staff meeting.

Because Jessica's school has a strong culture of collaboration, teachers were more than happy to share with their colleagues at staff meetings. The only requirement was that the strategy had to be shared in five minutes or less and could be easily replicated by any teacher on campus. They kept the Five-Minute PD idea focused on the interactive whiteboards at their staff meetings that school year to keep the learning momentum, but in digestible learning chunks.

Keep in mind that some of your staff members may hesitate at the idea of sharing their strategies because they may feel the strategy is not a big deal or exciting. It is your job as the leader to help them see how great their idea or strategy is and how impactful it can be to their colleagues once they learn about it. The idea/strategy does not need to be fancy, complicated, or take hours to prepare; it needs to be a quick, high-impact, low-preparation strategy.

ROUND ROBIN PD

Implementation Scenario: This is a great strategy to use when you want your team to bring strategies to share that revolve around a particular school or district focus.

This strategy is a modified version of the round robin reading strategy we may have participated in as students, where we take turns reading a passage aloud, with each student reading a small section at a time.

1. Ask each teacher/staff member to bring an example of a quick, impactful instructional delivery strategy (i.e., close reading, guided reading strategy, math fluency game, etc.), classroom management tool, family communication idea, etc.
2. In groups of 3–4 from different grade levels, departments, schools, etc., direct staff to take turns sharing one at a time. Ensure you allocate enough time for every person in the small group to be able to share.

Here, too, you can leave it up to the staff member to decide what they want to share, or you can choose to ask staff members to bring a strategy that directly connects to a school-wide or district-wide initiative.

EDCAMP-STYLE UNCONFERENCE

Implementation Scenario: Use when you want to make professional development relevant to what teachers need at that moment.

At a traditional edcamp-style conference, attendees are encouraged to propose sessions or topics for discussion, and the schedule is created on the spot, based on the interests and needs of the participants. You can re-create this same scenario at your school sites and in your district. It is an informal approach that focuses on collaborative learning and sharing.

Jessica was the chair of the Assistant Principal Academy for a couple of years. She planned one of her meetings to be structured in exactly this format. This format is a great way to promote engagement and collaboration among team members. This approach to learning and professional development is based on the principles of collaboration, active learning, and community building. What made this style of meeting so successful was that her team was flexible with the schedule and it allowed for attendees to move between groups as they see fit. This type of unstructured meeting fosters community building.

It was so well received by the assistant principals that they requested they have more meetings structured in the edcamp-style. They were able to come together to learn from one another, problem-solve together, and grow as professionals around topics that were relevant and important to them. The same can happen for teachers and classified staff as well. All you need is a space that is flexible and responsive to the needs and interests of the staff. There is no right or wrong way to do this; you just need to be able to let go of the control and allow your team to guide their own learning.

BREAKOUT SESSIONS

Implementation Scenario: This type of meeting can be particularly effective when the school or district has identified specific areas of focus or initiatives that need to be addressed or when teachers and staff have expressed interest in particular topics or areas of professional development. It's a powerful way to provide targeted, relevant, and engaging professional development for teachers and staff in a way that empowers them to take ownership of their own learning.

Using the breakout sessions strategy gives teachers and staff choice in what they want to learn for that day. Breakout sessions are predetermined and shared with staff prior to the staff meeting so that they have time to think about what session(s) they would like to attend and to ensure the session presenters have ample time to prepare. The breakout sessions offered will vary from school to school and must be relevant and meaningful to the needs of your team, school, and district.

Breakout sessions take planning. You can structure the breakout sessions to focus on school-wide and district-wide initiatives and/or you can ask for input a few weeks prior to the staff meeting regarding topics of interest. You can then work with your team to determine who could facilitate the session and/or if outside support is needed to facilitate the session.

Depending on how much time you have available for your staff meeting, you will need to determine how many session rotations you can schedule. For example, if you only have one hour available, you might consider having two twenty-minute session rotations to account for transition time and whole-group gathering before and after the sessions if you choose. Staff would then be able to attend two different sessions during your staff meeting time.

When Allyson plans breakout sessions, she sends out a quick survey to staff to ask them what they are interested in learning and which topic they would be willing to teach colleagues. She then uses this information to set up the breakout sessions so they are especially meaningful to staff and empower teachers as leaders.

TYING IT ALL TOGETHER

- Collaborative learning promotes strong, positive relationships within schools, departments, districts, and other organizations.
- Collaborating on new ideas and learning together is an effective way to strengthen relationships and improve the school as a whole.
- Learning together as a team can lead to a more cohesive, effective, and efficient team.

- Drawing upon the knowledge and expertise of internal staff fosters a collaborative culture that can drive positive changes in student learning and instructional practices.

Your Next Steps to Learning Together

Who are some experts on your staff?

_____

_____

_____

_____

_____

What topics might you tap staff to lead instructional meetings around?

_____

_____

_____

_____

When you center staff members as PD leaders, how can you present them in a way that leaves other staff feeling empowered, rather than playing the comparison game?

_____

_____

_____

_____

CHAPTER 7

Data Reflections and Problem-Solving

> *If we have data, let's look at data. If all we have
> are opinions, let's go with mine.*
>
> —JIM BARKSDALE

We have a love–hate relationship with data. We love it when it shows that our students are growing academically and affirms our instructional approaches. We hate it when it appears that all our hard work is not paying off. It can feel like an unfair judge of the strides we see our students making, and it can bring on tears of frustration at staff meetings. The good news is that there are strategies and approaches that can help data feel more like a friend than a foe.

"What does the data say?" is one of the most important questions we can ask each other during collaboration. Referencing data can feel like unlocking a mystery to increased student achievement. Collective efficacy is created when we explore student achievement together, share what is working, and reflect what is not working. Whether we call this time PLC time or data collaboration, the goal is the same: to work together to maximize student achievement through best practices. And it can be fun and rewarding!

To help guide the conversation and make informed decisions, it is important to use protocols and goals that are driven by data. Data can provide a reliable and objective perspective that can help to inform the discussion. Data can be numerical, such as numbers and types of discipline referrals or frequency charts, or it can be observational, such as reflecting on previous successes. On one hand, data can be seen as objective and a reflection of what is, rather than how we feel about a situation. On the other hand, data can conflict with the growth we are observing in the classroom. Utilizing a variety of data points can help bridge that gap.

Data plays a vital role in many of the decisions we make, and it can come in various forms, such as informal surveys or evaluations using a rubric. By using data as a reference, we can make more objective and unbiased decisions, as it helps to ground our thinking and remove personal biases and emotions from the problem-solving process. Data acts like a neutral party in the decision-making process, helping to ensure that we make more accurate and informed choices. In that context, it's important to present data as another collaborator in the room that helps to ground our thinking and ensures that we make more accurate decisions. And when we use engaging protocols that elevate all voices in an environment of collaboration, digging into data for action planning can be fun, too!

Data is like a trusted friend you turn to who always gives reliable and solid guidance and advice. Still, diving into data can be very emotional because teachers are passionate about student achievement and feel a deep sense of personal responsibility for their success. For example, turning to data can be especially helpful when we need to discuss complicated, fraught, or personal topics. Just like with achievement data, discussing metrics around student behavior can bring along big feelings, especially in a staff meeting. Data discussions can be hard, but we can do hard things together with appropriate trusting relationships and by thoughtfully using data in discussions and planning.

When presenting data that may be emotional, it can be helpful to utilize a strategy to help staff members process the data before the meeting.

> Data discussions can be hard, but we can do hard things together with appropriate trusting relationships and by thoughtfully using data in discussions and planning.

- Emailing the data out for staff to review before the meeting allows teachers to process their initial thoughts about the data on their own before discussing it with their colleagues, but only do this if they are able to accurately interpret the data on their own. When we use this strategy, we typically send the data out just one or two days before the meeting so most of the discussion can happen openly when we are all together.

- We know our staff members well, and we know who might be especially sensitive about particular data. For instance, if one grade level did not perform as well on the state assessment as the others, or one teacher typically gets emotional during data chats, it may be helpful to talk through the data in a personal conversation before the meeting.

- Another strategy that may help staff process the data before the meeting is to give them the first few minutes of meeting time to look over the data individually. They could even do this right in their own classrooms.

- Remind teachers that Dr. Douglas Reeves teaches us that we are not individually responsible for the data. What we are responsible for is what we **do** with the data.

FAST AND CURIOUS

Implementation Scenario: This activity is useful for approaching potentially fraught data with a more open-ended and neutral mindset of curiosity that suspends judgment.

A play on the popular movie series, Fast and Curious is like speed dating with data. Teachers will quickly review the data and then quickly summarize their interpretation. As they pass the data and summaries around, they will be able to learn from each other as they process the information the data provides. The activity ends with reflecting, using the Pause and Ponder strategy that can lead to action planning based on the teachers' input.

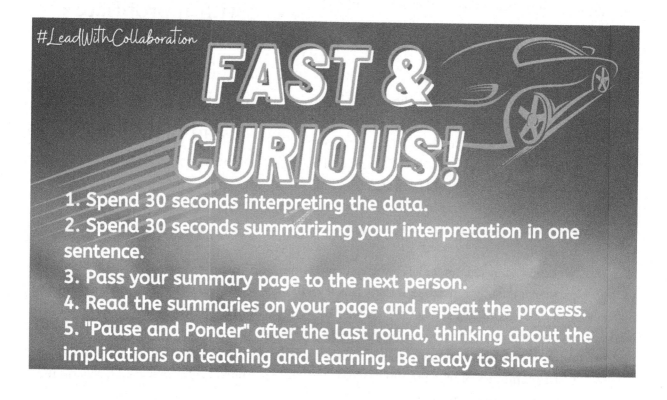

#LeadWithCollaboration

FAST & CURIOUS!

1. Spend 30 seconds interpreting the data.
2. Spend 30 seconds summarizing your interpretation in one sentence.
3. Pass your summary page to the next person.
4. Read the summaries on your page and repeat the process.
5. "Pause and Ponder" after the last round, thinking about the implications on teaching and learning. Be ready to share.

HIDDEN GEMS

Implementation Scenario: Use this activity when there's either a lot of positive news to celebrate or when you want to help staff frame mixed news in a positive light.

In this activity, we are going on a data treasure hunt. You can either post the data on a screen or give individual copies of the data to staff electronically or on paper. Once the data is made available, ask staff to perform the following steps:

1. Spend five minutes looking over the data to find the hidden gems: specific areas where student achievement shines.
2. Jot your "hidden gems" down on your paper.
3. Take the next two minutes to write an overall reflection.
4. Find a birthday month partner and share your gems and reflection. One person shares and the other responds, and then the roles reverse.
5. With your partner, come up with one diamond to share with the group.
6. When prompted, circle up with your partner to hear all the diamonds.
7. Pause and Ponder: How might we use our "hidden gems" reflection to help all student achievement shine bright? Based on the data, what area needs the most polishing?
8. Use the ideas generated during Pause and Ponder to create an action plan to guide teaching and learning. Each teaching team may make their own instructional plan, or you may create a whole-school plan. Note the use of the term "instructional" rather than "independent practice"; this plan will be to provide additional, different instruction to help students achieve learning goals.

Hidden Gems
A data treasure hunt!

Data: Date:

3 Hidden Gems:

Overall reflection:

 Partner Diamond Discovery:

Pause and Ponder:
What learning needs polishing?

VERTICAL ALIGNMENT VOYAGE

Implementation Scenario: Vertical alignment is important to make sure there are not learning gaps from year to year. This activity uses data in the form of student work samples.

Staff meeting time is a great time to support grade-level teams in creating vertical alignment plans. There are many ways to create vertical alignment plans, and we are going to share a unique twist on this idea that we have used with staff. You can choose any math or ELA content standard for this activity.

1. Select a content strand for the activity. Ask teachers to bring student work samples for that particular standard, making sure that they bring examples of students who are demonstrating mastery, below mastery, and exceeding mastery.
2. Prepare a slide that includes the particular content standard across all grade levels in the school. You will display this slide during the meeting so teachers can see the progression of the skill through the years.
3. Now it is time to take the "voyage"! Grade-level teams collaborate to chart a course of action to help their students get ready for the next level of learning. They take a peek at the "compass": their standards and the destination, which is what mastery looks like in the next grade level. The final step is to "set your course" by creating an action plan to support student learning. Visit leadwithcollaboration.net to access a slideshow template for this activity.

VERTICAL ALIGNMENT VOYAGE

 <u>Compass:</u> The standards both below, at, and above your grade level point you in the right direction.

 <u>Navigation Map:</u> Study what mastery looks like in the next grade level to get a clear picture of your destination.

 <u>Set Your Course:</u> Make a grade-level action plan to support your students in the next step according to the compass and navigation map.

#LeadWithCollaboration

IDEA SHOPPING

Implementation Scenario: Use this activity to help staff brainstorm ideas to problem-solve a concern. Data presented for this activity could be observational or assessment data.

Idea Shopping is a simple yet effective brainstorming technique that promotes a sense of agency and encourages the exploration of various options. It involves sharing and recording ideas without any judgment, and then selecting a few for further consideration and creating a plan based on one of them. This process is similar to shopping, where we deliberately examine different choices before making a decision.

1. Prior to the meeting, draw a shopping tag on the board or chart paper, or you can access a reproducible form at leadwithcollaboration.net. If you are collaborating digitally, you can put the form on a Jamboard or slide. At the top of the tag, list the behavior goal for the student (or the group of students) that you developed based upon observational data, behavior referrals, or a functional behavior analysis.

2. Assign roles for idea recorder, timekeeper, and facilitator. The facilitator will support the group in following the Idea Shopping guidelines. (2 minutes)

3. Share the guidelines for the five-minute idea share: all ideas are good ideas, no discussion about any of the ideas presented is allowed at this time, silence is okay because it is thinking time, and all ideas are phrased positively. (2 minutes)

4. During the five-minute idea share, ALL ideas are listed in the shopping tag. (5 minutes)

5. After all ideas are shared, each group member gets two "coins" (sticker dots or drawn dots) to put next to the ideas they would like to explore further. The group identifies the top 2–3 ideas using this method. The staff member who will be implementing the idea has final say on which one to move forward with. (5 minutes)

6. Develop an action plan to implement the idea, identifying who is responsible for each part of the action plan. (6 minutes)

Idea Shopping

ALL IDEAS WELCOME, THE MORE CHOICES THE MERRIER!

ACTION PLAN

ACTION STEP	RESOURCES NEEDED	STAFF RESPONSIBLE

#LeadWithCollaboration

SUCCESS SESSION

Implementation Scenario: This is great for building a positive mindset and emphasizes the efforts teachers have already made to improve the situation.

Many teachers who seek assistance with managing difficult behaviors may feel like they have failed. Often, they are presented with numerous suggestions for improvement that don't consider the efforts they have already made. As a result, they may leave feeling demoralized, which is not the desired outcome. This protocol prioritizes celebrating successes before addressing any challenges. The data used for the Success Session are the previous successes. For example, if teachers are struggling with students disrupting direct instruction, they will bring ideas for addressing this problem that have worked in the past. Or, if teachers are struggling with fitting in small-group instruction, teachers will bring examples of ways they worked small-group instruction into their schedule. The successes that teachers share will drive the action plan.

1. Before the meeting, let participants know that the focus of the meeting will be sharing successes they have had with this particular situation or any similar situations. This allows staff to think through any successes prior to the meeting.
2. The meeting begins with the Pause and Ponder strategy, and staff members write down successes they have had in the past with similar situations.
3. Going around the room, everyone shares at least one success and can share more if they would like.
4. Ask the group, "What can we learn from these successes to help us move forward?" Give everyone a chance to share their thoughts.
5. If necessary, at this point you can move into a brainstorming protocol (like Idea Shopping). Or, if the team is ready, you can select an idea to move forward with as part of an action plan.
6. Create an action plan for the 2–3 ideas that will be implemented. List the resources needed for each action item and which staff member will be responsible. Additionally, determine the start date for each action item.

TYING IT ALL TOGETHER

- Data is essential in decision-making and problem-solving as it helps remove personal biases and emotions from the process.
- By utilizing data in Professional Learning Communities or Data Teams, teachers can work collaboratively to improve student achievement through best practices.
- Staff meetings can foster a PLC culture through data discussions and planning.
- Collaboration is important when addressing behavior challenges, and specific protocols can facilitate structured discussions in a group setting.

Your Next Steps to Diving into Data Reflections

What difficult conversations or ideas might be facilitated by bringing in data as a collaborator?

_____

_____

_____

_____

_____

_____

_____

_____

What tools could you use to generate data about your school's needs?

_____

_____

_____

_____

_____

_____

_____

_____

_____

PART 3

ENDING WITH ACTION AND INSPIRATION

CHAPTER 8

Concluding with Clarity and Inspiration

> *The best way to succeed is to have a specific intent, a clear vision, a plan of action, and the ability to maintain clarity.*
>
> —STEVE MARABOLI

How we conclude our meetings can be even more significant than how we begin them. It is important for our team members to feel motivated, heard, valued, and energized after a meeting. The conclusion of the meeting isn't just a chance to remind staff of their importance and purpose; it's also an opportunity to get your team excited and looking forward to the next meeting.

Ending a meeting with inspiration can have several benefits. For one, it can help to boost morale and motivation among team members as well as create a positive team dynamic. When people feel inspired, they are more likely to be engaged and motivated to take action. Ending a meeting on a positive note can also help to build teamwork and a sense of community, especially when different departments or grade-level teams, or those working remotely, do not interact frequently.

Unfortunately, the crucial step of concluding with clear next steps is sometimes skipped in order to save time. Without clear next steps, though, team members may leave with different ideas of what was discussed and what actions need to be taken. If clear next steps are not established, it can lead to confusion and feel like wasted time and effort, potentially hindering the achievement of the goals that were set during the meeting. Without closure to a meeting, we run the risk of things being left unchallenged, unclear, and/or uncommitted.

At the end of a staff meeting, always make sure to:

- review action items and clarify any misunderstandings
- schedule follow-up meetings if needed
- review key points
- express gratitude to team members for their participation and contributions

> Without closure to a meeting, we run the risk of things being left unchallenged, unclear, and/or uncommitted.

By outlining clear next steps at the end of a meeting, team members will feel more confident and have a clear understanding of their responsibilities. With this clarity, team members will feel motivated and focused on achieving their goals, and you'll keep the momentum going to take action after leaving the meeting. That focused energy helps to keep everyone on the same page and moving in the same direction.

CLARITY ROUNDTABLE

Implementation Scenario: This strategy will help make sure everyone is on the same page without putting anyone on the spot.

This strategy was shared by Dr. Gracie Branch, associate director of professional learning at the National Association of Elementary School Principals (NAESP). She uses this strategy to confirm that staff members understand the content and next steps, and to address any lingering misunderstandings or questions.

1. Circle up in groups of 4–5 participants.
2. Direct group members to go around the circle and complete statements like:
   - "I'm going to leave today thinking about..."
   - "My understanding of our next steps is..."
   - "One question I still have is..."
3. Set aside a few minutes for the groups to confirm their understanding or address any misunderstandings among themselves.
4. Once groups are done talking among themselves, ask each group to share one or two points with the larger group.

You can vary the exercise by having participants write their responses down before discussion. If there are any unresolved questions, make a note of them and follow up with an email or bring the answers to the next staff meeting.

SUMMARIZE IT

Implementation Scenario: This strategy will be helpful to ensure that everyone is on the same page regarding project goals, next steps, and timelines. Team members will collaborate on a shared understanding statement that reflects everyone's input.

1. Using collaborative learning technology platforms such as Mentimeter, Google Slides, Google Jamboard, Padlet, etc., ask table groups to develop a short summary of their understanding of the meeting's focus and the next steps.

2. When groups are done discussing matters, direct one member of the group to add that short summary to the technology platform for the larger group to read.

3. All together, briefly discuss the ideas that have been posted. This gives colleagues the opportunity to collaborate on a shared understanding statement.

CHEER IT OUT

Implementation Scenario: This activity can be used when a new group needs to laugh together; the cheer will take on new meaning over the course of the year.

Laughing through the discomfort of a team cheer can help colleagues bond with one another, even if it feels awkward at first. Business consultant, entrepreneur, and author Cameron Herold says, "No matter how strange or embarrassing it seems at first, make sure everyone cheers at the end of the huddle. This will feel awkward at first, but everyone will grow to love it. The power of a good cheer will get people pumped to take on the workday."[1] This strategy may not be for everyone or every team, but give it a try. You'll be surprised by how much fun adults can have with this.

Having staff members who are particularly creative and outgoing lead the cheer can make it even more meaningful and enjoyable for the team. Huddles can help to create a positive work environment and are definitely worth trying out. This can strengthen team bonds in a classroom, school, or district office setting. You won't regret giving it a try!

VALUE ADDED

Implementation Scenario: When you want to encourage team members to recognize and validate the value that their colleagues have contributed to the conversation, this strategy will remind everyone that the time spent together was valuable.

Rarely is time taken to reflect on the value created by the discussion, decisions, and input given during the staff meeting. Taking time to reflect on the value of what was accomplished in the meeting allows for staff to feel validated as individuals and contributors.

In order to maximize a meeting's impact, you must get specific on the value that was added by individuals. For example, instead of saying, "Great work today, team," you can say something like, "Think of one staff contribution that resonated with you or that you feel should be highlighted and be ready to share it out with a colleague and/or the whole group."

---

1   Herold, Cameron. "The Format of a Productive Huddle." Accessed August 31, 2021. https://cameronherold.com/blog/huddle/.

SPARKING HOPE

Implementation Scenario: This is a great strategy when you want to end the meeting by acknowledging the struggle but leave with hope in your heart.

This activity helps staff understand the power of hope and leave the meeting with a spark of hope. Use an article such as "The New Science of Hope" by Dan J. Tomasulo, which was published in *Psychology Today*.[2] In the article, Dan shares the benefits of having high levels of hope and three simple ways to spark hope in your life. You can find a slideshow with a summary of the article by visiting leadwithcollaboration.net. After reading the article or discussing the slideshow, staff members will use the Pause and Ponder strategy to share their spark of hope.

READ-ALOUD

Implementation Scenario: When you want to end on a high note before a break, at the start or end of a new quarter, semester, or school year, or when a new school or district initiative is feeling overwhelming, a read-aloud can be very impactful.

Never underestimate the power of a read-aloud. If you have never read aloud to your staff, you should try it! This can be done throughout the year. There is no right or wrong time of the year to include a read-aloud as an inspirational end to a meeting. You determine when that timing could be.

Jessica took this inspiring ending a step further by sending her staff off with a copy of a book to add to their classroom libraries. Below are a few inspirational read-aloud titles you may want to consider:

- *Because I Had a Teacher* by Kobi Yamada: A great read to remind staff of the impact they make on students' lives.
- *Maybe* by Kobi Yamada: This book reminds us that *we matter*. It helps us reflect on our purpose and potential. It will remind us that we are the only us there ever has been or ever will be and that we need each of us on the team.
- *The Boy, the Mole, the Fox and the Horse* by Charlie Mackesy: It's a perfect book to read during uncertain times. It's a book that offers words of love and encouragement to feel heard and understood. It reminds us about the power of kindness and compassion.
- *The Oldest Student: How Mary Walker Learned to Read* by Rita Lorraine Hubbard and Oge Mora: It's an inspirational story of Mary Walker, a woman whose long life spanned from the Civil War to the civil rights movement, and who—with perseverance and dedication—proved that you're never too old to learn. This is a great book to read to remind staff that we never stop

---

2   Tomasulo, Dan J. "The New Science of Hope." *Psychology Today.* Accessed February 5, 2023. https://www.psychologytoday.com/us/blog/the-healing-crowd/202207/the-new-science-hope.

learning and that what they do day in and day out matters. When addressing school literacy initiatives, consider adding this read-aloud to the end of your meeting.

- *Because You Are My Teacher* by Sherry North: This story demonstrates the significant role teachers play in the lives of their students and how learning can be an exciting adventure.

POSITIVE POSTCARDS HOME

Implementation Scenario: This strategy can be used to promote a positive classroom culture, foster relationships between teachers and students, and show students that their hard work and efforts are appreciated.

One of Jessica's favorite ideas to incorporate into a staff meeting is allocating a few minutes for teachers to write a positive postcard to their students. She ordered custom postcards and had the secretary print student address labels for each class roster. The goal is for each student to receive a postcard from their teacher or other staff members by the end of the school year. Jessica made it easy for her team by providing the postcards and address labels, and by collecting the postcards to be mailed out the next day. Receiving a personalized card in the mail from a teacher or staff member can be very meaningful for a student, showing them that their hard work is appreciated. Ending a staff meeting with an actual positive note helps remind the team that their work matters and that we are here to make positive impacts in students' lives.

TYING IT ALL TOGETHER

- Ending the meeting with clarity helps to maintain momentum, keep everyone on the same page, and avoid confusion or misunderstandings.
- Without clear next steps, meetings can feel like wasted time and effort, hindering the team's ability to achieve its goals.
- The conclusion of a staff meeting is an important opportunity to motivate and energize team members.
- Ending with inspiration is especially important when different departments or teams do not interact regularly.

Your Next Steps to Concluding with Clarity and Inspiration

What recent initiatives would benefit from added momentum?

What would be the result of dedicating time at the end of your next staff meeting to provide clarity and inspiration? How might it impact the outcome of your next meeting?

CHAPTER 9

Keeping the Focus Beyond the Meeting

> *Diligent follow-up and follow-through will set you apart from the crowd and communicate excellence.*
>
> —JOHN C. MAXWELL

We've all left meetings feeling good about what we discussed only to later wonder what happened to the ideas we talked about and the next steps we were going to take. Where did that momentum and excitement go?

All too often, the collaborative and productive conversations that happen during a staff meeting end up going nowhere. After leaving the meeting, teachers' attention shifts to a new set of priorities as they are running off to get ready for the next day, to get home to their families, or to return emails and phone calls. With the strategies from the previous chapter, we know that staff members are leaving the meeting with clarity and inspiration. However, if there is not a plan for keeping the focus beyond the meeting, the clear plan forward becomes quite gray and foggy.

Following through with action plans is crucial in effective collaboration. It also contributes to a cultural environment of accountability. As Aristotle said, "A promise made must be a promise kept." For trusting relationships to be developed and maintained, there must be confidence that every member of the team will fulfill their promises. In a staff meeting, our promise is the clear action plan we leave with. We keep our promises in between the meetings by following through with our parts. We develop faith in each other through clear communication about our progress and next steps.

This chapter includes tips and ideas about how to keep the focus beyond the staff meeting. From thorough meeting notes to follow-up strategies, there are measures leaders can take to ensure that the progress made at the meeting continues and that promises are kept.

> Following through with action plans is crucial in effective collaboration.

MEETING MINUTES

Implementation Scenario: This is great for keeping everyone accountable and making sure details don't fall through the cracks.

This tip seems like a no-brainer, but we know that meeting minutes are often nonexistent or far from comprehensive.

First things first, the person responsible for taking meeting minutes cannot be the meeting facilitator. Both of us have made this error and have tried to do it all during staff meetings, and it simply is not effective. Sharing responsibilities during staff meetings contributes to a culture of collaboration. Capitalize on staff member strengths by carefully matching your goals for meeting minutes with a staff member who will take better notes than you ever could.

Another important part of the meeting minutes is sharing them right after the meeting along with the meeting action plan. If you want to have a bit of fun with the name for your minutes, you could consider "Collaboration Chronicle" or something aligned with your staff meeting name.

COLLABORATION ROADMAP

Implementation Scenario: This strategy is a great way to keep momentum up toward specific goals.

We love including the word *collaboration* anywhere we can, and this roadmap is essentially the action plan for moving forward with the decisions and plans that were made during the staff meeting. Important components of the roadmap include the specific action items, the resources needed, the staff responsible, and the anticipated implementation date.

We created a template you can use, or you can create your own. This is designed to be shared with everyone who attended the meeting and to be followed up on at the next staff meeting. You may want to select one staff member to be responsible for the minutes and another to be responsible for documenting the action plan.

Collaboration Roadmap

ACTION ITEM	RESOURCES	STAFF	DATE

#LeadWithCollaboration

FREQUENT CHECK-INS

Implementation Scenario: This would be a useful strategy for school or district leaders when they need to track the progress of ongoing projects or initiatives.

As educators, we are aware of the positive impact of regular check-ins with our students. They allow us to give them additional support, track their progress, and make real-time adjustments that enhance their learning. As school leaders, scheduling check-ins for action items can be a valuable tool.

Check-ins can be performed by the leader or a staff member who is particularly adept at them. The designated staff member can give updates on the progress of the action items and any extra resources needed.

Pro tip: Schedule the check-ins on your Google Calendar right after the meeting, and invite staff responsible for the action items on the calendar event.

REPLY ALL

Implementation Scenario: A great way to keep collaborations and conversations going in between meetings.

Our love–hate relationship with "reply all" is mostly hate, isn't it? But this feature can be put to good use following a staff meeting by encouraging staff members to use it for sharing their thoughts. They can share feedback on the meeting, the steps to be taken based on the action plan, or a major point to take away.

It's important to explain the goal of this approach before the meeting ends so that staff members are aware of what they can expect.

1. Send a follow-up email after the meeting that summarizes an action step or topic.
2. Ask teachers to "reply all" within a certain timeframe. For instance, you may ask them to share their key takeaway from the meeting within the next forty-eight hours.
3. Teachers share their takeaway, an idea they will implement, or their next steps so all of their colleagues can learn from them.
4. This can happen immediately after the meeting, or can be especially powerful a few days or even a week later.

THE YEAR IN REVIEW

Implementation Scenario: Great for when you want to reflect on what you've accomplished as a team.

One of Allyson's favorite things to do is to save up all the staff meeting agendas and post them around the room for the last staff meeting of the school year. She writes out each meeting's agenda on chart paper so it is easy to save them in her office as the year progresses.

It is fun to take a trip down memory lane together, and it is an important reminder of all they accomplished together that year. This activity also helps inform next steps in their learning and progress, and those next steps can be incorporated into the staff meeting plan for the next school year.

1. In small groups (Allyson randomly assigns them), staff travel around to the different agendas.
2. They first discuss the impact the meeting had on their classroom practices, each taking a turn to share.
3. Then they each list a next step for the particular agenda focus.
4. They record their thoughts on another piece of chart paper that is posted next to the agenda.
5. The last group shares the most powerful impact and key next steps with the whole group.

FIVE-STAR RATING

Implementation Scenario: This can be useful in improving the effectiveness of future staff meetings.

Asking your staff to rate the meeting and give feedback can help a leader strengthen and improve future staff meetings. It can be a little intimidating to have your team rate the meeting and give you feedback, but it will show you how the team is experiencing staff meetings and allow you to improve.

Letting your staff rate the meeting will give you insight on how valuable your team feels staff meetings are and how they are being managed. It's also a great way to gain a clear understanding of what works well and areas for improvement.

Soliciting and recording feedback could be as simple as having staff add sticky notes to a poster with their written feedback, or you could use tech like Google Forms to collect anonymous feedback. You can set up Suggestion Boxes in a common area, such as the staff lounge, and encourage staff members to drop in anonymous feedback forms after meetings. This provides a physical way for staff members to provide anonymous feedback and can be especially useful for staff members who may not feel comfortable using online tools.

The team will feel valued for being asked their opinion. Time is valuable, so ensure you are creating the best possible experience for your team while they are there. Shoot for that five-star rating!

ONGOING ACTIVITIES FOR KEEPING MOMENTUM HIGH BETWEEN MEETINGS

GLIMMERS

Implementation Scenario: This idea can encourage staff to look for the glimmer in their day.

This idea was adapted from Jennifer Nickel, an elementary principal in Indiana. For this activity, you need a designated wall or bulletin board (preferably in a communal staff area) and sticky notes.

1. Encourage staff to write at least one "glimmer" for each day (some days are harder than others) and add them to the Happy Wall for others to read.
2. At the end of a quarter or semester, bring all those sticky notes to a staff meeting for the team to read back through. This idea can be replicated in classrooms with students, just like it was at Jennifer Nickel's school.

WEEKLY STAFF SHOUT-OUTS

Implementation Scenario: This idea is great for recognizing ongoing achievements and for teammates to highlight one another.

This can be done digitally or using hard copies. Using Google Forms, we provided a spot in the weekly bulletin for staff to submit shout-outs for their colleagues. Every shout-out was added to the next weekly bulletin for all to read. This activity could be adapted using physical staff shout-out cards that can be pinned to a designated location for all to see or announced in weekly, daily, or social media announcements.

THANK-YOU CARD STATION IN THE STAFF LOUNGE

Implementation Scenario: Similar to the Letter-Writing Party card idea, a thank-you card station can be set up in the staff lounge to be utilized by all team members throughout the school year. It makes writing a thank-you card to a colleague quick, easy, and accessible.

TYING IT ALL TOGETHER

- A common problem in meetings is when attendees leave feeling good about what was discussed, but later forget what was discussed and what the next steps were.
- Action plans and follow-up strategies are crucial for effective collaboration and building a culture of accountability.
- By keeping promises made in meetings and clear communication about progress and next steps, leaders can ensure that progress made during the meeting continues.
- The tips, strategies, and ideas shared in this chapter can keep the focus beyond the staff meeting and contribute to trusting relationships among staff members.

Your Next Steps to Keeping the Focus Beyond the Meeting

What Keeping the Focus Beyond the Meeting ideas might you want to try at your next staff meeting?

_____

_____

_____

_____

_____

_____

_____

_____

_____

How might you empower others and delegate responsibilities for action plan follow-through?

_____

_____

_____

_____

_____

_____

_____

_____

_____

CONCLUSION

You Are Ready to Lead with Collaboration!

> *None of us, including me, ever do great things. But we can all do small things, with great love, and together we can do something wonderful.*
>
> —MOTHER TERESA

The research is clear: we need each other in order to help our students achieve. It also feels right when we are moving forward as a team, all headed in the same direction. As educators, it is in our nature to help others grow and succeed, and this applies to our relationships with students and with our colleagues. We are excited to be on this journey to transform staff meetings to create a culture of collaboration together.

Why collaboration? Although there are numerous aspects beyond our control, we can organize interactive, cooperative, and purposeful staff meetings that will enhance various facets such as efficiency, interaction, originality, inventiveness, increased job satisfaction, and involvement.

To summarize, here are some guidelines to keep in mind from each of the nine chapters:

1. Taking the time to prepare for a successful meeting will pay off in dividends. Organizing an agenda can help structure the meeting, while careful planning of the physical meeting space is essential for success. Additionally, considering the meeting space as a means of creating a particular experience that supports the desired outcomes is crucial. Mentally preparing for the meeting is equally vital as creating a clear agenda and selecting an appropriate meeting space.

2. All staff members deserve to feel valued and included in our meetings. To start the school year or when there are new staff members, icebreakers may be helpful, but intentional inclusion activities are more effective throughout the rest of the year. Meeting leaders should carefully select activities that are comfortable for staff and be clear about the purpose of the activity.

3. Students thrive when teachers work as a team rather than as a group. Transforming groups into teams takes more than just conventional team-building activities; it requires building trust among colleagues and cultivating a collective efficacy mindset to enhance student achievement. It is essential to assess the specific needs of the staff and transparently communicate the goals and objectives of team-building activities.

4. Creating a culture of appreciation motivates people to perform at their best. Celebrating successes, big or small, can help achieve that. Setting a positive tone by incorporating celebrations at the beginning of meetings reminds team members of the value of their contributions, and expressing gratitude and celebrating achievements during meetings can lead to increased dedication and effort, fostering a positive work environment. Simple gestures can go a long way in making staff meetings enjoyable and conducive to team success.

5. It is vital to ensure that all learning and collaboration is meaningful, even if the topics may seem mundane. Although "mundane" topics like reviewing policies and handbooks are important to include, they can be made more engaging and collaborative through the use of technology tools or creative activities, transforming them into magical opportunities for collaboration.

6. Through learning together, teams can become more effective and efficient. Leveraging the expertise of staff can foster a collaborative culture that drives positive changes in instructional practices and student learning outcomes. Encouraging collaborative learning in schools and organizations can enhance relationships by promoting teamwork and knowledge sharing.

7. Utilizing data is crucial in decision-making and problem-solving. Professional learning communities (PLCs) can use data collaboratively to improve student achievement through best practices, and staff meetings can foster a PLC culture through data discussions and planning. Specific protocols can facilitate structured discussions in a group setting and help address behavior challenges collaboratively.

8. It is essential to end meetings with clarity and a shared understanding of next steps. Without clear action items, meetings can feel like wasted time and hinder the team's ability to achieve its goals. Moreover, the conclusion of a staff meeting provides a valuable opportunity to inspire and energize team members, especially when different departments or teams do not interact regularly.

9. Leaders can keep the focus beyond the staff meeting by keeping promises made in meetings and maintaining clear communication about progress and next steps. To ensure that progress made during meetings continues, action plans and follow-up strategies are crucial for effective collaboration and building a culture of accountability.

We have provided you with a variety of strategies, activities, and tips to support collaboration, and now we are offering one more tool to add to your tool belt: a template for planning effective staff meetings. You can access a digital version of the template by visiting www.leadwithcollaboration.net.

When planning your next staff meeting, keep in mind that the agenda should be guided by the goals for the collaboration. If you do not have specific goals to achieve, there is no need for a meeting. Once you have established the collaborative purpose of the meeting, you can craft an agenda that maximizes time for the best outcome. One way to do this is to start the meeting with the main portion, such as Diving into Content, and then use opening activities, setup, communication, and the closing to support your goals.

#LeadWithCollaboration

Staff Meeting Planning Template

Date/Time of Meeting:			
Collaborative Purpose of Meeting:			
Meeting Components	Action Plan	Resources Needed	Timeline
Agenda Communication *How will you involve staff in creating the agenda & communicate it ahead of time?*			
Physical Setup *How will the setup contribute to the purpose of the meeting? How will staff feel welcome and ready to collaborate?*			
Opening Activity *Inclusion, energizer, mindful, or grounding*			
Diving into the Content *What strategy or activity will help staff collaborate and grow together?*			
Concluding with Clarity and Inspiration *How will the ending provide clarity and empower teachers?*			
Keeping the Focus Beyond the Meeting *What is the plan for creating and implementing an action plan?*			

Our template includes space to provide information on the activity, resources required, and a timeline to help you plan the meeting in an efficient manner. Do not hesitate to repeat successful strategies or activities. While introducing new activities can engage the team, effective strategies can be reused multiple times. You can make slight changes to keep it fresh, but do not discard a strategy or activity that has been beneficial for your team in the past.

Even though the work we do can be challenging, it doesn't mean we can't enjoy learning and growing together. If you and your team are having fun, it will create a more positive and engaging environment. We recommend that you review your agenda and identify the parts that can be fun. If you find that it lacks fun elements, try to incorporate them and make it interactive. A simple activity like tossing a ball around while staff members share their reflections can make the meeting livelier and more enjoyable. Remember, just like in the classroom, if you bring the energy, the staff will follow.

> Remember, just like in the classroom, if you bring the energy, the staff will follow.

We all understand that time is valuable and should not be wasted on unproductive meetings that do not foster collaboration. Just like planning effective instruction for students in the classroom, planning effective professional development and collaboration for staff is a significant undertaking. We hope that this book will serve as a useful guide for planning and conducting successful staff meetings that contribute to a culture of collaboration and trust. Additionally, we hope that it will inspire your own creativity as you develop strategies and activities. We are keen to learn from you and encourage you to share your ideas on social media and tag us (@AllysonApsey and @MrsJessGomez) using our hashtag #LeadwithCollaboration.

The staff meeting transformation gifts will keep coming! Please scan the QR code or visit leadwithcollaboration.net to sign up for our email list. We will update you with new ideas, inspiration, and leadership fun throughout the year.

Acknowledgments

Allyson and Jessica agree that they could not lead without the support they get at home from their family. They would like to acknowledge their families for everything, from the encouragement they provide, to sharing the household responsibilities, to inspiring them to become the best versions of themselves.

Jessica and Allyson are passionate about being connected educators, both at home and far away. They would like to thank the educators they have worked alongside and the educators who motivate them across the country. We can do so much more when we work together, and they want to acknowledge the energy, ideas, and gifts that other educators have shared with them.

Finally, a special thank you to the team at Dave Burgess Consulting, Inc. Your dedication to lifting the voices of practitioners is unmatched. We are so thankful for your support of this project, and for making the dream of writing this book come to life.

About the Authors

Allyson Apsey is an educational leader focused on creating need-satisfying school environments for students and staff where they feel seen and valued. She has taught grades three through eight and has been an award-winning principal for all levels K–12 in addition to serving as a district leadership coach. Recognizing the significant impact trauma has had on many of our students, staff, and families, Allyson became a Certified Trauma Practitioner in Education. The support provided to students affected by trauma is beneficial to all students because it is grounded in strong, positive relationships based on trust. Allyson has also served as a leader at the state level through her work with the Michigan Elementary and Middle School Principals Association (MEMSPA) as a member of the Executive Board of Directors.

Allyson shares her passion for helping everyone discover the best in themselves through her blog, *Serendipity in Education*. She has authored several books, including *Lead with Collaboration: A Complete Guide for Transforming Staff Meetings*, *Leading the Whole Teacher*, and *The Path to Serendipity*. She has written two books to share the serendipity message with children, the picture book *The Princes of Serendip*, and a middle-grade chapter book called *The Serendipity Journal*. She has been published in *Principal* magazine and was featured in a TEDx Talk called "Serendipity Is Everywhere."

After serving as a state, school and district leader for nineteen years, Allyson now travels the country to work with educators from coast to coast. She is an associate with Creative Leadership Solutions, where she works with districts and schools across the nation to improve performance at every level from the classroom to the boardroom with evidence, passion, and results.

She also loves speaking to passionate groups of educators to spread the #SerendipityEDU message and to inspire others to create environments where educators and students can thrive. You can connect with Allyson on Twitter, Instagram, and Facebook at @AllysonApsey, through her website, AllysonApsey.com, or via email at AllysonApsey@gmail.com.

Jessica Gomez is an educational leader who has served as a teacher, principal, and district level director. Her experiences as an educator, second language learner, and child who experienced poverty inspire her passion to intentionally embed people-first practices into the work she does. Jessica is the 2021 Association of California Superintendents and Administrators (ACSA) Region 12 Elementary Principal of the Year, serves on the Future Ready Schools® (FRS) Advisory Board for the principal strand, is a Fellow for the National Association of Elementary School Principals (NAESP) Center for Women in Leadership, and has served as a Mentor for NAESP's Aspiring Principals Academy.

Jessica is an associate with Creative Leadership Solutions, where she supports school leaders on building relationships with colleagues, project management, time management, and organizational effectiveness and works with school teams to improve performance at all levels.

Jessica is a presenter, professional developer, coach, and mentor. Her drive and passion for leadership work have led her to thrive in transforming school cultures and climates. Jessica is a transformational leader who inspires educators across the nation to develop as leaders, risk takers, innovators, and champions in breaking down barriers of poverty and inequity through standards, instruction, and assessment alignment work. She is passionate about equity and closing opportunity gaps for historically underserved students.

Jessica is a lifelong learner who believes in the power of being a connected educator by building Professional Learning Networks (PLNs) across the country. You can connect with Jessica on Twitter or Instagram @MrsJessGomez or via email at mrsjessgomez@gmail.com.

Bring Allyson and Jessica to Your School or District

You will not find a more charismatic or engaging pair of educational leaders than Allyson and Jessica! If you are looking to support leaders to engage educators in collaboration, or if you are looking to support teachers to engage students in empowering and collaborative ways, you won't want to miss out on the opportunity to invite Allyson and Jessica to your school or district.

They offer half-day, full-day, or multi-day workshops where leaders and teachers will leave inspired and with an action plan to create a culture of collaboration in their district, school, or classroom.

Contact them at allysonandjessica@gmail.com
Contact Jessica Gomez at mrsjessgomez@gmail.com
Contact Allyson Apsey at allysonapsey@gmail.com

More from

Dave Burgess Consulting, Inc.

Since 2012, DBCI has published books that inspire and equip educators to be their best. For more information on our titles or to purchase bulk orders for your school, district, or book study, visit DaveBurgessConsulting.com/DBCIbooks.

MORE FROM THE *LIKE A PIRATE*™ SERIES

Teach Like a PIRATE by Dave Burgess
eXPlore Like a PIRATE by Michael Matera
Learn Like a PIRATE by Paul Solarz
Plan Like a PIRATE by Dawn M. Harris
Play Like a PIRATE by Quinn Rollins
Run Like a PIRATE by Adam Welcome
Tech Like a PIRATE by Matt Miller

LEAD LIKE A PIRATE™ SERIES

Lead Like a PIRATE by Shelley Burgess and Beth Houf
Balance Like a PIRATE by Jessica Cabeen, Jessica Johnson, and Sarah Johnson
Lead beyond Your Title by Nili Bartley
Lead with Appreciation by Amber Teamann and Melinda Miller
Lead with Culture by Jay Billy
Lead with Instructional Rounds by Vicki Wilson
Lead with Literacy by Mandy Ellis
She Leads by Dr. Rachael George and Majalise W. Tolan

LEADERSHIP & SCHOOL CULTURE

Beyond the Surface of Restorative Practices by Marisol Rerucha
Change the Narrative by Henry J. Turner and Kathy Lopes
Choosing to See by Pamela Seda and Kyndall Brown
Culturize by Jimmy Casas
Discipline Win by Andy Jacks
Escaping the School Leader's Dunk Tank by Rebecca Coda and Rick Jetter
Fight Song by Kim Bearden
From Teacher to Leader by Starr Sackstein
If the Dance Floor Is Empty, Change the Song by Joe Clark
The Innovator's Mindset by George Couros

It's OK to Say "They" by Christy Whittlesey
Kids Deserve It! by Todd Nesloney and Adam Welcome
Leading the Whole Teacher by Allyson Apsey
Let Them Speak by Rebecca Coda and Rick Jetter
The Limitless School by Abe Hege and Adam Dovico
Live Your Excellence by Jimmy Casas
Next-Level Teaching by Jonathan Alsheimer
The Pepper Effect by Sean Gaillard
Principaled by Kate Barker, Kourtney Ferrua, and Rachael George
The Principled Principal by Jeffrey Zoul and Anthony McConnell
Relentless by Hamish Brewer
The Secret Solution by Todd Whitaker, Sam Miller, and Ryan Donlan
Start. Right. Now. by Todd Whitaker, Jeffrey Zoul, and Jimmy Casas
Stop. Right. Now. by Jimmy Casas and Jeffrey Zoul
Teachers Deserve It by Rae Hughart and Adam Welcome
Teach Your Class Off by CJ Reynolds
They Call Me "Mr. De" by Frank DeAngelis
Thrive through the Five by Jill M. Siler
Unmapped Potential by Julie Hasson and Missy Lennard
When Kids Lead by Todd Nesloney and Adam Dovico
Word Shift by Joy Kirr
Your School Rocks by Ryan McLane and Eric Lowe

TECHNOLOGY & TOOLS

50 Things to Go Further with Google Classroom by Alice Keeler and Libbi Miller
50 Things You Can Do with Google Classroom by Alice Keeler and Libbi Miller
140 Twitter Tips for Educators by Brad Currie, Billy Krakower, and Scott Rocco
Block Breaker by Brian Aspinall
Building Blocks for Tiny Techies by Jamila "Mia" Leonard
Code Breaker by Brian Aspinall
The Complete EdTech Coach by Katherine Goyette and Adam Juarez
Control Alt Achieve by Eric Curts
The Esports Education Playbook by Chris Aviles, Steve Isaacs, Christine Lion-Bailey, and Jesse Lubinsky
Google Apps for Littles by Christine Pinto and Alice Keeler
Master the Media by Julie Smith
Raising Digital Leaders by Jennifer Casa-Todd
Reality Bytes by Christine Lion-Bailey, Jesse Lubinsky, and Micah Shippee, PhD
Sail the 7 Cs with Microsoft Education by Becky Keene and Kathi Kersznowski
Shake Up Learning by Kasey Bell
Social LEADia by Jennifer Casa-Todd
Stepping Up to Google Classroom by Alice Keeler and Kimberly Mattina
Teaching Math with Google Apps by Alice Keeler and Diana Herrington

Teachingland by Amanda Fox and Mary Ellen Weeks
Teaching with Google Jamboard by Alice Keeler and Kimberly Mattina

TEACHING METHODS & MATERIALS

All 4s and 5s by Andrew Sharos
Boredom Busters by Katie Powell
The Classroom Chef by John Stevens and Matt Vaudrey
The Collaborative Classroom by Trevor Muir
Copyrighteous by Diana Gill
CREATE by Bethany J. Petty
Deploying EduProtocols by Kim Voge, with Jon Corippo and Marlena Hebern
Ditch That Homework by Matt Miller and Alice Keeler
Ditch That Textbook by Matt Miller
Don't Ditch That Tech by Matt Miller, Nate Ridgway, and Angelia Ridgway
EDrenaline Rush by John Meehan
Educated by Design by Michael Cohen, The Tech Rabbi
The EduProtocol Field Guide by Marlena Hebern and Jon Corippo
The EduProtocol Field Guide: Book 2 by Marlena Hebern and Jon Corippo
The EduProtocol Field Guide: Math Edition by Lisa Nowakowski and Jeremiah Ruesch
The EduProtocol Field Guide: Social Studies Edition by Dr. Scott M. Petri and Adam Moler
Empowered to Choose: A Practical Guide to Personalized Learning by Andrew Easton
Expedition Science by Becky Schnekser
Frustration Busters by Katie Powell
Fully Engaged by Michael Matera and John Meehan
Game On? Brain On! by Lindsay Portnoy, PhD
Guided Math AMPED by Reagan Tunstall
Innovating Play by Jessica LaBar-Twomy and Christine Pinto
Instructional Coaching Connection by Nathan Lang-Raad
Instant Relevance by Denis Sheeran
Keeping the Wonder by Jenna Copper, Ashley Bible, Abby Gross, and Staci Lamb
LAUNCH by John Spencer and A.J. Juliani
Learning in the Zone by Dr. Sonny Magana
Lights, Cameras, TEACH! by Kevin J. Butler
Make Learning MAGICAL by Tisha Richmond
Pass the Baton by Kathryn Finch and Theresa Hoover
Project-Based Learning Anywhere by Lori Elliott
Pure Genius by Don Wettrick
The Revolution by Darren Ellwein and Derek McCoy
The Science Box by Kim Adsit and Adam Peterson
Shift This! by Joy Kirr
Skyrocket Your Teacher Coaching by Michael Cary Sonbert
Spark Learning by Ramsey Musallam

Sparks in the Dark by Travis Crowder and Todd Nesloney
Table Talk Math by John Stevens
Unpack Your Impact by Naomi O'Brien and LaNesha Tabb
The Wild Card by Hope and Wade King
Writefully Empowered by Jacob Chastain
The Writing on the Classroom Wall by Steve Wyborney
You Are Poetry by Mike Johnston

INSPIRATION, PROFESSIONAL GROWTH & PERSONAL DEVELOPMENT

Be REAL by Tara Martin
Be the One for Kids by Ryan Sheehy
The Coach ADVenture by Amy Illingworth
Creatively Productive by Lisa Johnson
Educational Eye Exam by Alicia Ray
The EduNinja Mindset by Jennifer Burdis
Empower Our Girls by Lynmara Colón and Adam Welcome
Finding Lifelines by Andrew Grieve and Andrew Sharos
The Four O'Clock Faculty by Rich Czyz
How Much Water Do We Have? by Pete and Kris Nunweiler
P Is for Pirate by Dave and Shelley Burgess
A Passion for Kindness by Tamara Letter
The Path to Serendipity by Allyson Apsey
Recipes for Resilience by Robert A. Martinez
Rogue Leader by Rich Czyz
Sanctuaries by Dan Tricarico
Saving Sycamore by Molly B. Hudgens
The Secret Sauce by Rich Czyz
Shattering the Perfect Teacher Myth by Aaron Hogan
Stories from Webb by Todd Nesloney
Talk to Me by Kim Bearden
Teach Better by Chad Ostrowski, Tiffany Ott, Rae Hughart, and Jeff Gargas
Teach Me, Teacher by Jacob Chastain
Teach, Play, Learn! by Adam Peterson
The Teachers of Oz by Herbie Raad and Nathan Lang-Raad
TeamMakers by Laura Robb and Evan Robb
Through the Lens of Serendipity by Allyson Apsey
The Zen Teacher by Dan Tricarico
Write Here and Now by Dan Tricarico

CHILDREN'S BOOKS

The Adventures of Little Mickey by Mickey Smith Jr.
Alpert by LaNesha Tabb

Alpert & Friends by LaNesha Tabb

Beyond Us by Aaron Polansky

Cannonball In by Tara Martin

Dolphins in Trees by Aaron Polansky

I Can Achieve Anything by MoNique Waters

I Want to Be a Lot by Ashley Savage

The Magic of Wonder by Jenna Copper, Ashley Bible, Abby Gross, and Staci Lamb

Micah's Big Question by Naomi O'Brien

The Princes of Serendip by Allyson Apsey

Ride with Emilio by Richard Nares

A Teacher's Top Secret Confidential by LaNesha Tabb

A Teacher's Top Secret: Mission Accomplished by LaNesha Tabb

The Wild Card Kids by Hope and Wade King

Zom-Be a Design Thinker by Amanda Fox